D1620172

Basil Tozer

The Horse In History

ISBN/EAN: 9783337365066

Printed in Europe, USA, Canada, Australia, Japan

Cover: Foto ©ninafisch / pixelio.de

More available books at **www.hansebooks.com**

THE

HORSE IN HISTORY

BY

BASIL TOZER

AUTHOR OF
"PRACTICAL HINTS ON RIDING TO HOUNDS" ETC.

WITH TWENTY-FIVE ILLUSTRATIONS

METHUEN & CO.
36 ESSEX STREET W.C.
LONDON

First Published in 1908

INTRODUCTORY NOTE

AFTER directly helping on the progress of the world and the development of civilisation almost from the time when, according to Nehring's interesting studies, the wild and primitive horses of the great Drift began to exhibit distinct differences in make, shape and individual characteristics, the horse has reached the limit of its tether.

For with the dawn of the twentieth century, and the sudden innovation of horseless traffic, any further influence that it might have exercised upon the advancement of the human race comes rapidly to a close.

That the horse's reign is over—though it is sincerely to be hoped that horses will be with us still for many years—the statistics issued recently by our Board of Agriculture in a measure prove. For in those statistics it is stated that the number of horses in the United Kingdom decreased during last year alone by no less than 12,312, and later statistics show that the decrease still continues.

In the following pages, therefore, the writer has striven to trace the progress of the horse from very early times down to the present day mainly from the standpoint of the effect its development had upon the advancement of the human race. For this reason though a selected number of the most famous horses that lived in the centuries before Christ, and between the time of Christ and the period of the Norman Conquest, and that have lived within the last nine centuries, have been mentioned, the horses of romance and mythology have for the most part been passed over.

Every effort has been made to obtain information that is strictly accurate, a task of no small difficulty owing to the mass of contradictory evidence with which the writer has found himself confronted in the course of his researches. To the best of his ability he has winnowed the actual facts from the mass of fiction that he has come upon in the writings of some of the earlier historians, and to some extent in records, manuscripts and private letters of more recent times to which he has had access.

B. J. T.

BOODLE'S CLUB, 1908.

CONTENTS

PART I

FROM VERY EARLY TIMES TO THE CONQUEST

CHAPTER I

CHAPTER II

PART II

FROM THE CONQUEST TO THE STUART PERIOD

CHAPTER I

CHAPTER II

CHAPTER III

CHAPTER IV

PART III

FROM THE STUART PERIOD TO THE PRESENT DAY

CHAPTER I

CHAPTER V

LIST OF ILLUSTRATIONS

17

SOME WORKS CONSULTED

OF the many volumes the writer has consulted whilst engaged in compiling this book, the following are among the more important. The list is arranged alphabetically, according to the authors' names. To the authors or editors, as the case may be, and to the publishers of these works, the writer here begs to acknowledge his very deep indebtedness for the assistance he has derived from consulting the volumes named.

ARRIAN (F.)—"The Anabasis of Alexander."

AUREGGIO (E.)—"Les Chevaux du Nord de l'Afrique."

AZARA (F. DE)—"The Natural History of the Quadrupeds of Paraguay and the River La Plata."

BERENGER (R.)—"The History and Art of Horsemanship."

BLOUNT (T.)—"Antient Tenures."

BLUNT (W. S.) "Bedouin Tribes of the Euphrates."

BOUSSON (M. A. E.)—"Etude de la Représentation du Cheval."

CHARRAS (J. B. A.) "Histoire de la Campagne de 1815."

CHOMEL (C.)—"Histoire du Cheval dans l'antiquité et son rôle dans la civilization."

CHURCH (A. J.)—"Roman Life in the Days of Cicero."

COOK (T. A.)—"The History of the Turf," and "Eclipse and O'Kelly."

DARWIN (C. R.)—"Variation of Animals and Plants."

ERMAN (A.)—"Life in Ancient Egypt."

EWART (J. C.)—"The Multiple Origin of Horses and Ponies"; "A Critical Period in the Development of the Horse"; and "The Penicuik Experiments on Breeding between Horses and Zebras."

FITZWYGRAM (Sir F. W. J.)—"Horses and Stables."

FLOWER (Sir W. H.)—"The Horse."

GAST (E.)—"Le Cheval Normand et ses Origines."

GILBEY (Sir W.)—"Horses Past and Present," and "The Great Horse, or War Horse."

GREENWELL (W.)—"British Barrows."

HADDON (A. C.)—"The Study of Man."

HALL (H.)—"The Horses of the British Empire."

HAYES (M. H.)—"Points on the Horse."

HOLM (A.)—"The History of Greece."

HORE (J. P.)—"History of Newmarket."

HUME (D.)—"Imperial History of England."

HUME (D.)—"The History of the House of Douglas."

JONSON (B.)—"The Alchemist."

JOWETT (B.)—"Thucydides."

LODGE (E.)—"Illustrations of British History."

MAYNE (C.)—"Odes of Pindar."

MITCHELL (T.)—"The Comedies of Aristophanes."

MONTFAUCON (B. DE)—"Antiquities."

MORGAN (H.)—"The Art of Horsemanship."

MURRAY (D).—"Life of Joan of Arc."

NEWCASTLE (DUKE OF)—"Observations on Horses."

PETRIE (F.)—"History of Egypt."

PIETREMENT (C. A.)—"Les Chevaux dans les Temps Historiques et pré-Historiques."

PLUTARCH—"Life of Alexander the Great."

PRESCOTT (W. H.)—"The Conquest of Mexico."

REYCE (R).—"Breviary of Suffolk."

RIDGEWAY (W.)—"The Origin and Influence of the Domestic Horse," and "The Early Age of Greece."

RUSKIN (J.)—"The Queen of the Air."

SCHLIEBEN (A.)—"The Horse in Antiquity."

SIDNEY (S.)—"The Book of the Horse."

SOTHERBY (W.)—"Georgics of Virgil."

19

Southey (R.) — "Iliad of Homer."

Street (F.) — "The History of the Shire Horse."

Strutt (J.) — "Sports and Pastimes of the People of England."

Tasso (T.) — "Jerusalem Delivered."

Taunton (T.) — "Famous Horses."

Trimmer (Mrs M.) — "Natural History."

Tweedie (Mrs Alec.) — "Hyde Park: Its History and Romance."

Tweedie (W.) — "The Arabian Horse."

Upton (Capt. R. D.) — "Newmarket and Arabia."

Vaux (Baron C. M. de) — "A Cheval. Etude des Races Françaises et Etrangères."

White (C.) — "History of the Turf."

Witt (C.) — "The Trojan War."

Yule (Sir H.) — "Marco Polo."

Standard classics consulted have for the most part been omitted from this list. The writer wishes in addition to thank his friend, Dr William Barry, the distinguished classical scholar, for the trouble he has taken in helping to revise some of the earlier of the proof sheets; Professor William Ridgeway, of Cambridge, the famous historian and archæologist, for letters containing advice that has proved of use; Mr Theodore Andrea Cook, the most trustworthy authority we have upon the history of the Turf and the modern thoroughbred, for letters of introduction, etc.; and the Directors of the British Museum and the Directors of the National Gallery for allowing photographs to be taken for reproduction. For the sake of convenience the centuries b.c. are alluded to in the same way that centuries a.d. are alluded to, that is, one century in advance. Thus 550 B.C. is spoken of as the fourth century B.C.; 250 a.d. as the third century A.D., and so on.

THE HORSE IN HISTORY

PART I

FROM VERY EARLY TIMES TO THE CONQUEST

CHAPTER I

THOUGH according to the more trustworthy of our
naturalists hoofed animals do not occur until the Tertiary
Period in the history of mammals, there can be no doubt
that from an epoch almost "so far back that the memory of
man runneth not to the contrary," in the literal meaning of
that legal phrase, the horse has played a prominent part in
the development of the human race.

Reference is made incidentally to "the horses of Abraham"
by the author of a historical novel published recently; but
then even the most pains-taking of writers of fiction is apt
to err in minute points, and can one blame him when the
lands over which he travels, and the subjects of which he
treats, are so numerous and vary so widely? For we know
from Genesis—also from certain other later sources that may
be depended upon for accuracy—that though the prophet
had creatures of divers kinds bestowed upon him, yet the
horse probably is one of the few animals he did not receive.

Many of the important and famous victories won by
Rameses—Sesostris as the Greeks termed him—and by other
monarchs of the eighteenth and nineteenth dynasties, most
likely would have proved crushing defeats but for the

assistance they obtained from horses. As it happened, however, Rameses—whom recent writers declare to have been a very barefaced "boomster"—succeeded with the help of his horses in marching triumphant through many of the outlying territories in Africa as well as in Asia.

We have it on the authority of Professor Flinders Petrie and other distinguished historians that Aahmes I.—a king of the seventeenth dynasty who drove out the Hyksos— reigned from 1587 to 1562 B.C., and chariots do not appear to have been used in Egypt prior to his accession.

Indeed, as Professor Owen himself has pointed out, horses are not found represented on any of the monuments of the very early Egyptians, so that apparently the Egyptians of the eighteenth dynasty, whose monuments probably are the first to show horses and chariots, must have been the first to turn their attention seriously to the employment of horses for useful purposes.

And yet from further statements made in Genesis it seems certain that a native Egyptian king who flourished somewhere about the time of Jacob—that is to say between 1800 and 1700 B.C.—owned many horses and chariots. The Egyptians apparently did not mount horses until a very late period in their history, and even the chariots they constructed were, until many years had passed, used only in time of war. The lower classes, if one may call them so, used only the ass, a beast that must have been popular amongst the Egyptians for centuries before horses were even heard of in Egypt.

From Genesis we gather too that Pharaoh made Joseph drive in his second chariot; but the Egyptians who bought corn from Joseph and gave horses in exchange for it belonged probably to the well-to-do class that in time of war was compelled to provide the king with almost as many horses and chariots as he needed, or at any rate as many as he asked for.

In the records of Babylonia it is stated that horses were first employed in the great city about the year 1500 B.C. The Libyans, however, must have broken horses to harness some centuries before this, and indeed learnt to ride them with some skill, for it is proved beyond all doubt that the women of Libya rode horses astride at any rate so far back as the seventeenth century B.C., and that in addition to this horses were at about that time being driven in pairs by the Libyans, to whom even the four-horse chariot cannot have been quite unknown.

It has not been proved, from what I have been able to ascertain, that in Neolithic times horses were already tamed, but some remains of horses discovered at Walthamstow, in Essex, are said to date back approximately to that period and to indicate for that reason that horses were domesticated in the Neolithic Age.

Evidence does exist, however, that in the Neolithic and Bronze Ages horses of a type that closely resembled that of the horses of the Palæolithic Age were to be found in several parts of Europe. The Trojans, as most of us know, bred horses very largely indeed, so much so that we read of King Erichthonius, who in the thirteenth century B.C. was in his heyday, that he became "richest of mortal men" and the possessor of "three thousand mares which pastured along the marsh meadow, rejoicing in their tender foals," a statement that indirectly recalls the fine lines in Longfellow's "The Minnisink":

> "They buried the dark chief—they freed
> Beside the grave his battle steed;
> And swift an arrow cleaves its way
> To his stern heart! One piercing neigh
> Arose,—and on the dead man's plain
> The rider grasps his steed again."

Erichthonius, according to Virgil, was the first to handle a four-in-hand, for in the third book of his "Georgics" we are told how

> "Bold Erichthonius first four coursers yok'd
> And urg'd the chariot as the axle smok'd."

Rather a risky proceeding and one from which we may conclude that bold Erichthonius would have flouted the axiom promulgated recently by the more prudent members of a well-known coaching club that "no team ought to be driven faster than ten miles an hour, upon an average"!

━━━━━━━━━━

Though allusions to the horse are made repeatedly in the Bible, they give us little or no insight as to the horse's influence upon the nations and their development. The notorious steed of Job that when among the trumpets exclaimed "Ha! Ha!" and then winded the battle afar off and fretted itself unduly upon hearing "the thunder of the captains and the shouting" has been described by several writers, but no two descriptions appear to tally.

Solomon, according to the "Book of Kings," must have owned quite a large stud, for we read that he had horses brought out of Egypt, and that a chariot came up and went out for six hundred shekels of silver, a horse for a hundred and fifty, "and so for all the kings of the Hittites, and for the kings of Syria, did he bring them out." The Hittites, whom

Professor Jensen assures us were Indo-Europeans, are also shown to have had horses when they made their way into Northern Palestine, probably at some period prior to 1400 B.C., but trustworthy information about the horses and how the Hittites treated them is not obtainable.

As for the horses in the Mycenean Period—the Bronze Age of Greece—the monuments of that epoch bear testimony to the esteem in which they were held. The indigenous people of Greece were presumably the Pelasgians, and these monuments remain to bear testimony that such a people once existed.

In a like manner do the gravestones of the Acropolis of Mycenæ bear indisputable evidence, for upon three of them at least are to be seen sculptured in low relief a chariot, a pair of horses, and a driver, the date of this particular sculpture being approximately the fourteenth century B.C.

It seems practically beyond dispute that before the year 1000 B.C. no people rode on horseback except the Libyans, though chariots must have been used quite 2000 years before that. Yet by the time Homer wrote his poems horsemanship was becoming common amongst a section of the Greeks.

Indeed by that time feats of skill on horseback upon a par with the antics we see performed to-day in circuses were at least known, and probably they were often watched and greatly liked. Listen, for instance, to the following Homeric simile—the translation is almost literal:—

"As when a man that well knows how to ride harnesses up four chosen horses, and springing from the ground dashes to the great city along the public highway, and crowds of men and women look on in wonder, while he with all confidence, as his steeds fly on, keeps leaping from one to another."

There are two references at least in Homer to "four male horses yoked together," but the practice of driving four-in-hand certainly was not common in the eighth century B.C., or probably until long after. The above reference, however, to feats of skill performed on horseback, recalls to mind a story, probably more or less true, that has to do with the luxurious people of Sybaris, in Southern Italy.

In the early centuries before Christ, so it is related, this people trained all its horses to dance to the sound of music, to the music of flutes in particular. The inhabitants of Croton having heard of this, and being sworn enemies of the Sybarites, determined to take advantage of the information and attempt to conquer their foe with the aid of strategy.

For this reason they provided all the musicians in their own army with flutes in place of trumpets and the other instruments they had been in the habit of using, and then without delay declared war upon the Sybarites.

The latter, to do them justice, responded at once, in spite of the condition of lethargy to which the life of luxury they had been leading was supposed to have reduced them. No sooner did they approach the Crotonian lines, however, than "a great part of the army," as we are told, "set up a merry tune," which had the effect of stampeding the Sybarites' horses, for "they instantly threw off their riders and began to skip and dance."

As a natural consequence the Sybarite army was taken at a disadvantage and quickly routed with great slaughter, "very many horses being killed during the engagement, to their owners' dismay and grief."

─────────────

This strange story may be in a measure exaggerated, but probably it is based on truth, in which case it proves that the Greeks of Magna Græcia at any rate made use of cavalry before the rest had attempted to do so. Also we know that in the year 510 B.C. the Crotonians destroyed Sybaris entirely.

The Assyrians too, at about this period, evidently had well-appointed cavalry, for Ezekiel speaks of their being "clothed in blue, captains and rulers, all of them desirable young men, horsemen riding upon horses," and goes on to give particulars which, in so far as they relate to the mode of life in vogue with these desirable young men, are calculated to shock the susceptibilities of prudish persons, and to amuse others.

In the light of the Higher Criticism Homer's "Iliad" is believed to have been written by various hands, and incidentally the Criticism throws useful light upon the horse in his relation to the history of the nations known to have flourished in the very early centuries before Christ.

One need not here describe such steeds as Agamemnon's mare, swift Æthe, that was given to him by his vassal, Echepolus of Sicylon, and subsequently driven in the chariot race by Menelaus; or Phallas, the horse of Heraclios; or the horses of the Pylian breed of which Homer speaks at length; or Galathe, Ethon, Podarge or any of the other steeds of which Priam's eldest son, "magnanimous and noble Hector," was so justly proud. Also the horses of mythology do not possess great interest for the majority of modern readers other than classical scholars.

That Homer himself, however, had sound knowledge of the qualifications which go to make up what in latter-day English we probably should term a "finished charioteer" is shown by the following rather well-known lines that here are translated almost literally: —

"But he who in his chariot and his steeds
Trusts only, wanders here and there
Unsteady, while his coursers loosely rein'd
Roam wide the field; not so the charioteer
Of sound intelligence; he, though he drive
Inferior steeds, looks ever to the goal
While close he clips, not ignorant to check
His coursers at the first, but with tight rein
Ruling his own, and watching those before."

Menesthus, emphatically one of the finest of the many fine riders spoken of in the "Iliad," or, as Homer himself describes him, "foremost in equestrian fame," is typical of the horsemen of that period.

In the "Iliad" too we find what I believe I am right in stating to be the first direct historical allusion to wagering on horse races. But the medium current on racecourses in those days was not coin. The odds apparently were laid in "kitchen utensils"—as a lad with whom I was at school once construed the line, to his subsequent discomfiture— namely, cauldrons and tripods.

Such, at least, we are led to infer from the paragraph in the twenty-third book of the "Iliad," which, according to William Cowper's blank verse translation, edited by Robert Southey, runs somewhat as follows: —

"Come now—a tripod let us wager each,
Or cauldron, and let Agamemnon judge
Whose horses lead, that, losing, thou mayst learn."

Or more euphoniously, as Lord Derby has it:

"Wilt thou a cauldron or a tripod stake
And Agamemnon, Atreus' son, appoint the umpire
To decide whose steeds are first?"

The cauldrons and tripods referred to were of course of great value, and, as trophies, highly prized by competitors in the races and other competitions calling for a display of skill and daring.

There is another allusion in the "Iliad" to the presentation of a tripod as a great reward for valour. It occurs in the eighth book, and the passage goes more or less like this:

"Let but the Thunderer and Minerva grant
The pillage of fair Ilium to the Greeks,
And I will give to thy victorious hand,
After my own, the noblest recompense,
A tripod or a chariot with its steeds,
Or some fair captive to partake thy bed."

I recollect how at school this passage, with several others, used to be rigorously excluded when Homer was being construed, with the result that Kelly's famous "Keys to the Classics" used afterwards to be produced surreptitiously, and the "censored" lines turned carefully into English.

──────────

From what Homer tells us elsewhere, and from additional sources, we may conclude that of all the races that bred horses and took just pride in them in the early centuries before Christ the Thracians were probably the most renowned.

The brilliant horsemanship of "noble Patroclus of equestrian fame," the amiable and staunch friend of Achilles, must not be passed unmentioned; nor the deeds of prowess that are attributed to Euphorbus, "famous for equestrian skill, for spearmanship, and in the rapid race past all of equal age"; nor yet the deeds of Hyperenor whose skill in handling horses may be likened to the skill of Rarey in our own time.

The following lines from the "Iliad" are of interest here because they serve to indicate to some extent the style of harness and useless trappings that must have been in vogue amongst the wealthy in Homer's day:—

"So Hera, the goddess queen, daughter of great Cronos, went her way to harness the gold-frontleted steeds; and Hebe quickly put to the car the curved wheels of bronze, eight spoked, upon their axletree of iron."

Then:

"Golden is their felloe, imperishable, and tires of bronze are fitted thereover, a marvel to look upon; and the naves are of silver, to turn about on either side. And the body of the car is plaited tight with gold and silver straps, and two rails run round about it.

"And a silver pole stood out therefrom; upon the end she bound the fair golden yoke, and set thereon the fair breast-straps of gold, and Hera led beneath the yoke the horses, fleet of foot, and hungered for strife and the battle-cry."

It has been argued that about the time of Homer gold and silver were deemed to be comparatively of small value, and that therefore the trappings described were not so costly as one naturally would conclude they must have been.

Upon this point opinions are about equally divided.

Professor Ridgeway tells us that by comparing the

31

foregoing description with actual specimens of chariots and horse trappings that have been found in Egypt we can form an accurate impression of the appearance that was presented by the original old chariots, and form also an idea of the way they were put together, while the plaiting with straps of gold and silver recalls at once the floor of the Egyptian chariot with its plaited leather meshwork—probably the forerunner of leather springs.

———————

Though Odysseus and Diomede are known to have mounted their Thracian horses, we have it on irrefutable evidence that at this period chariots were still generally used, so that most likely horses were ridden but seldom.

Indeed the Homeric poems provide us with probably as much authentic information as to the methods of managing and breeding horses that were in vogue in Greece, in Thrace, and in Asia Minor in the very early years before Christ, as any half-dozen other volumes put together that purport to deal with the ways and customs of a period of which, when all is said, little enough is known.

Naturally the Thracians had in those days some of the best horses that could be procured, while those they drove in their war chariots are said to have been quite unrivalled. That they possessed very many chariots is proved by Homer's realistic account of the slaying of Rhesus, the Thracian king, with a dozen or so of his bravest followers, and the episode in connection with that incident.

Indeed when Odysseus and Diomede had captured Dolon, the Trojan spy, the latter at once declared that there were "also Thracians, new-comers, at the furthest point apart from the rest, and amongst them their king, Rhesus, son of

Eioneus," adding that his were "the fairest horses that ever I beheld, and the greatest, whiter than snow, and for speed like the winds. His chariot too is fashioned well with gold and silver, and golden is his armour that he brought with him, marvellous, a wonder to behold."

Apparently most of the horses bred by the Acheans at about this time were either dun-coloured or dapple. *Xanthos* signifies Dun, and *balios* dapple; but then we have to remember that *xanthos* was used frequently to denote also the colour of gold.

Achilles' steeds were mostly dapple-dun, and they had more or less heavy manes. They belonged most likely to the breed so popular among the Sigynnæ of central Europe about the fifth century B.C. Certainly Homer makes it plain that in the early Iron Age horses were bred in many parts of Greece; that, though driving was a common practice, riding was indulged in but rarely; that cavalry in battle was quite unknown; and lastly that though the heroes, as they were called, fought mainly in chariots, the great body of the army consisted of well-trained infantry.

As time went on horsemanship apparently came to be appreciated more and more, for we read that about the year 648 B.C. — the thirty-third Olympiad — "a race for full-grown riding horses" was inaugurated in addition to the chariot races, and there appear to have been plenty of entries. Then though the war chariot had disappeared almost completely, before the outbreak of the Persian Wars, its place was not taken by well-appointed and well-equipped cavalry until some years later.

Though little attention need be paid to the Greek legend

that Pegasus was the first horse ever ridden—a legend not mentioned in Homer—it nevertheless is interesting to know that this historic animal was supposed to have been foaled in the Bronze Age, and in Libya. That naturally would have been prior to the arrival of the fair-haired Acheans from Central Europe, so one need not be astonished, as several writers obviously are, at finding that when these large-limbed Acheans first appeared the Greeks already knew how to ride.

At the same time they seldom did ride their dun-coloured little cobs, preferring, apparently, to drive them in pairs in chariots. That the Libyans were finished horsemen centuries before the Greeks learnt how to ride has already been mentioned; though whether or no the Greeks were first taught horsemanship by the Libyans is a question still debated by students of ancient history.

———

In the north-west of Asia Minor the Libyans had dark bay horses with a white star upon the forehead about the year 1000 B.C., and a hundred or so years later horses of this breed were largely imported into various parts of Asia Minor.

Indeed some of the more enthusiastic of the modern historians who have studied closely the descent of horses from generation to generation persist in maintaining that even in Great Britain and Ireland modern horses with this white star upon the forehead have in their veins some Libyan blood! How this can well be when we know almost without doubt that until towards the close of the Bronze or the beginning of the Iron Age the horse was hardly made use of at all by the inhabitants of these islands, I leave it to more learned men to decide among themselves.

It is remarkable that whereas from very early times horses of Asiatic-European breeds have proved more or less unmanageable except when bitted, the horses of Libya are known to have been controlled quite easily by nosebands only. Some of the nosebands, or rather halters, used in early times were made of plaited straw, and to-day halters of almost similar make and pattern are still employed in certain of the more remote parts of Ireland.

The bits found most suitable for Asiatic-European horses were made first of all of horn, then chiefly of bone, later of copper, and finally of bronze and iron. Homer, in his "Iliad," alludes to bits of bronze placed between the horse's jaws, and this probably is one of the first instances of literary evidence we have that a thousand years before Christ's birth horses were controlled by bits.

Of course Xenophon has much to say upon the question of bits and bitting, and his capital treatise on horsemanship throws valuable light also upon the horse in its relation to the history of that epoch, as we shall see. Upon one point in particular in this connection Xenophon lays great stress. He maintains it to be imperative that every horseman shall possess two bits for his horse or horses, one with links of moderate size, and one with sharp and heavy links, bidding us at the same time remember that "whatever sorts of bits be used, they should be flexible, for where a horse seizes a rigid bit he has the whole of it fast between his teeth ... but the other sort is similar to a chain, for whatever part of it be taken hold of, that part alone remains unbent—the rest hangs."

So that apparently bits single- and double-jointed, and therefore flexible, were used in the early Iron Age by the people of North-Western Europe.

COMBAT BETWEEN AMAZONS AND ATTIC HEROES. FOURTH
CENTURY, B.C.
From a Greek vase in the British Museum

By the beginning of the fourth century B.C. many, though not all, of the Greek and the Macedonian mounted soldiers had come to consider some sort of covering for the horse's back to be necessary to their equipment; and so long previously as the eighth century B.C. horse cloths had been adopted by the Assyrians, a people sufficiently wise to realise from the first that a horse with something on his back is more comfortable to sit upon than one without.

These early races probably would have employed cavalry several centuries sooner than they eventually did, but for the difficulty they experienced in arming themselves to their complete satisfaction when mounted. Such peoples, for

36

instance, as the Egyptians, the Assyrians, and the Greeks of the Mycenean or Bronze Age, habitually protected themselves with the aid of large and oblong shields when they fought on foot, but on horseback these shields proved cumbersome. Possibly that was the reason that when the Normans and other Teutonic races began to fight on horseback they so soon discarded their round and clumsy shields in favour of a shield broad at the top and tapering downward, the shape of shield we see on the Bayeux tapestry.

With regard to the war chariots in use before this time, we may be quite sure that even the very first employed had not wheels cut from solid blocks as some are represented as having, though possibly the most primitive of the agricultural chariots were so constructed.

For the rest, the early chariots of the Egyptians of the eighteenth dynasty, and in use in India under the Vedic Aryans, and amongst the Hittites, the Assyrians, the Persians, the Libyans, the Mycenean Greeks, the Homeric Acheans, the Gauls of Northern Italy and in Gaul itself; also among the ancient Britons and the early Irish, had wheels with a hub, a felloe, and spokes, the latter from four to twelve in number.

And inasmuch as this information bears indirectly upon the horse in his relation to early historical records, it is not out of place here.

To return again to the question of harness, we have it on the authority of Herodotus that "the Greeks learned from the Libyans to yoke four horses to a chariot," and we know already that before the time of Herodotus, who wrote in the fifth century B.C., the Greeks had found Libyans riding astride horses and driving sometimes two-horse and occasionally four-horse chariots. At that time—about 632

B.C.—the Greeks were planting Cyrene.

White horses were in ancient days at all times largely in demand among the people of the various nations; and while Pindar alludes incidentally to white horses being ridden by the Thessalians in his time, Sophocles, writing half-a-century or so later, describes a Thessalian chariot that was drawn by white horses.

One of the regions in which white horses were bred, probably in great numbers, was the banks of the Caspian where the River Bug flows from it, for Herodotus states clearly that "around a great lake from which the River Hypanis (called now the Bug) issued, there grazed wild white horses." Those particular animals possibly may have been in reality only tarpans in their winter coats, and not actually horses. The point has been argued more than once, but has never been quite settled. A white horse famous towards the close of the fifth or early in the fourth century was Kantake, of the notorious Prince Gautama, but nothing need be said about it here, trustworthy records being unprocurable.

The great cities of Magna Græcia—Sybaris, Tarentum, Croton, and so on—obviously had formidable cavalry in the sixth century B.C.; Sicily and Southern Italy being almost equally renowned for the riding horses obtainable there. The statagem to which the Crotonians had recourse in 510 B.C. to bring about the fall of Sybaris has been described, and it is said that for some years prior to the destruction of the city some five or six thousand of the inhabitants were in the habit of riding in procession on horseback upon the occasions of the great festivals held there.

CHAPTER II

AS we gradually approach the time of Christ we find increasing interest being taken in horses by the kings and great chiefs of different countries, for the value of cavalry in war was now quickly becoming manifest.

In the early days of the Homeric or Iron Age the Celts of Noricum and the Danube, though still retaining chariots, had begun to ride on horseback, and by the third century B.C. these Celtic tribes already possessed well-trained and very formidable cavalry. As a natural result the demand for still better horses grew steadily, and soon it became common to import horses into the Upper Balkan, and countries beyond the Alps, from the Mediterranean area.

Perhaps the best description of a chariot race at Delphi is to be found in the *Electra* of Sophocles—Sophocles flourished in the third century B.C. At about the same period Herodotus tells us that the Sigynnæ, the only tribe north of the Danube that he mentions by name, had "horses with shaggy hair five fingers long all over their bodies." These horses were "small and flat-nosed and incapable of carrying men, but when yoked under a chariot were very swift."

Consequently the natives drove them largely in chariots.

Though Herodotus does not allude to the colour of these small, flat-nosed horses, there is reason to believe that dun was the colour most prevalent at about this time. With regard to the horses of Northern Britain Dio Cassius says that two of the chief tribes—namely, the Caledonians and the Mæatæ—"went to war in chariots, as their horses were small and fleet," while when the Gauls passed into Italy, towards the beginning of the fourth century B.C., they drove chariots but did not ride, in which respect they resembled the Sigynnæ north of the Danube.

Thucydides, writing at the end of the third century B.C., speaks with interest on the subject of horses' hoofs, pointing out that the reason so many of the cavalry horses of the Athenians went lame towards the close of the Peloponnesian War was not that they had been wounded, as some historians have averred, but owing simply to their not being shod. This was after the Spartans had occupied Decelea and suffered their heavy loss.

Alcibiades, in the third century B.C., had many horses, and in the sixth book of "Thucydides" he tells us in his speech that he sent into the lists no less than seven chariots, adding that "no other man ever did the like"; and later he goes on to mention that he won the first, second and fourth prizes.

Apparently Alcibiades knew his world, and if so it would seem that his world was not unlike the world we know to-day, for in another passage he sententiously yet philosophically tells us that we "must not expect to be recognised by our acquaintance when we are down in the world; and on the same principle why should anyone complain when treated with disdain by the more fortunate?"

This particular sentence is according to the translation of "Thucydides" by the late Professor Jowett, who leaves us to infer what we please concerning the sociological views held by Alcibiades.

Among the first to employ war chariots with scythes intended to mow down the enemy were the Persians, if historical records are to be trusted, and we read that the chariots they used in the battle of Cunaxa, in 401 B.C., were provided with sharp blades, while in after years the people of Syria had war chariots with spears as well as scythes.

Thus in the bloody battle fought between Eumenes of Pergamus, and Antiochus of Syria, to mention but a single instance, Antiochus had four-horse chariots with scythes and spears in his front line of battle, whereupon Eumenes purposely "created terror" amongst these horses, with the result that they turned suddenly and dashed back into the lines of Antiochus, spreading devastation and death on all sides in their own ranks.

Certain it is that upon that occasion many horses were cut to pieces by the scythes, but for a full and graphic description of what happened I must refer the reader to the thirty-seventh chapter of the immortal "Livy."

The esteem in which horses, especially war horses, were held in the centuries that immediately preceded the coming of Christ may to some extent be gathered from the prominence accorded to them when coins to be used as the circulating medium began to come into general vogue. Thus on the first of the Carthaginian coins—they were struck in the third century B.C.—we find represented a horse upon one side, a palm-tree upon the other, while on the coins of the important Sicilian settlement, Panormus, a horse is shown.

I have tried to disentangle from a mass of only semi-trustworthy records the true origin of the well-known saying: "He has Seius' horse in his stable." So far as one can ascertain, it is traceable to the fates of the various ill-starred owners of the horses of Gnæus Seius, from Seius down to Anthony. Plutarch says that the famous Philip II. loved to commemorate his Olympian victories by stamping the figure of a steed upon some of his coins, and certainly he was devoted both to horses and horse racing. We read too that between 359 and 336 B.C. he entered both chariots and riding horses for the Olympian competitions.

GREEK COINS SHOWING HORSES IN THE EARLY CENTURIES BEFORE
CHRIST

*1, 3. Agrigentum. 2, 4, 5, 6, 7, 9. Syracuse. 8. Asia Minor and Greece. Philip of
Macedon. 10. Hellenestic period. Hiero of Sicily*

44

Similarly a proportion of the Sicilian coinage bore the impression of a horse, and many of the great chariot races are commemorated on coins. Several of the Agrigentine coins, for instance, show a quadriga driven by winged Nike, in commemoration probably of the victory of Exænetus, while some of the coinage of Syracuse dating back so far as 500 B.C., and even earlier, represents a four-horse chariot upon the face of the tetradrachms, and, on the didrachms, a man riding one horse and leading another. Some of the drachms show merely a man mounted.

Indeed we are told that Gela not only prided herself on her victories won on the race track, but upon what was, of course, of more importance—her splendid cavalry. A number of her coins represent a four-horse chariot, some a two-horse chariot, and occasionally a wounded foe being speared to death by a horseman, galloping or stationary. These coins probably are among the earliest of their kind ever struck.

The most ancient of all representations of Sicilian horses, however, which serve to prove that the Sicilians were beyond doubt a horse-loving race, is the quadriga on one of the metopes of the archaic temple of Silenus, believed to have been founded in 628 B.C.

While upon the subject of sculpture, casual reference must be made to the notorious Wooden Horse of Troy, described fully in Homer and alluded to centuries later by Virgil, the horse of which the famous sculptor, Strongylon, made a model in bronze towards probably the close of the fifth century.

The story of this horse hardly needs repetition, but briefly it is to the effect that soon after Hector's death Ulysses commanded Epeios to construct a wooden horse of great size that ostensibly was to be used as an offering to the gods to please them and thus ensure a safe voyage back to Greece.

Unsuspectful of treachery, the Trojans received the great effigy and brought it into their city; whereupon, in the dead of night, the Greek soldiers hidden within it crept cautiously out, pounced silently upon the Trojan guards and slew them before they could defend themselves; then opened the gates of Troy, let in their own soldiery, and finally set fire to the city.

Menelaus is said to have been among the Greeks concealed in the wooden horse.

If evidence in addition to that already given be needed to prove that the ancient Greeks held horses in high esteem, and that the Grecian conquests were probably in a great measure due to the help afforded by the possession of horses, notice has only to be taken of the vastness of the space occupied by the Athenian cavalry shown on the Parthenon frieze.

Indeed at about this period probably no accomplishment was quite so highly esteemed as horsemanship, with the result that the wealthy classes began to pay special attention to the training their sons received in it, while treatises were published upon the art and how best it might be acquired.

The first horsemen of whom we have indisputably authentic records invariably rode bareback, and, with the exception of the Libyans, used some sort of bit. According to Xenophon—and apparently no other historian of his time is so thoroughly to be trusted for strict accuracy—the Greeks of the fifth century B.C. were almost as fastidious upon the subject of bits and bittings as some hunting men of to-day are.

Some writers upon this subject have erred. Thus the impression is prevalent that the horses of the ancient Greeks were all much smaller than modern horses, and the steeds shown on the Parthenon frieze are sometimes said to afford proof that this was so. A proportion of the horses of those early times undoubtedly were smaller than the modern horse is, but on the other hand plenty were not. Probably the mistaken critics base their assertion upon the fact that the men shown on the Parthenon frieze and similar compositions, also on some of the vase paintings of that period, apparently are as tall as, or taller than, the horses beside which they are standing or on which they are mounted.

The reason men and horses are so represented simply is that according to a standard rule of ancient Greek art the heads of men and animals, and of all other figures shown on such compositions, must be as nearly as possible upon a level, even though some of the figures may be standing, some seated, some on horseback, some in chariots.

This rule, known as "Isokelismos," is of course in direct opposition to the rule of nature, yet as it existed it had to be observed, and therefore no attempt should ever be made to compare the height of men or beasts shown in such representations as the Parthenon frieze merely by the appearance and the proportions they present. By observing how far below the horses' bellies the feet of the mounted men hang, an approximate idea of the height of the men by comparison with that of some of their horses may be arrived at.

Herodotus is of opinion that about the year 480 B.C. finer horses were owned by the Nisæan than by any other people of Asia, and he mentions that white horses were so highly valued by the Persians of about that period—who are known to have used many white horses for sacrificial

47

purposes—that "some three hundred and sixty horses, or about one for every day in the year, and five hundred talents of silver," was the tribute sent by the Sicilians. This statement leads to the conclusion that white horses must have been exceptionally plentiful in the region.

That Armenia had many horses, which were largely used even so far back as the fifth century B.C., can be gathered from the writings of Ezekiel, for the prophet does not hesitate to declare that the people of Togarmah, which presumably was part of Armenia, traded in the fairs in horses and mules.

Pindar, who so glorified King Arcesilas, tells us that Cyrene became famous as the city of steeds and goodly chariots, and later the poet Callimachus sang of his home "famed for her steeds." Hiero II. of Syracuse owed practically all his great successes to the fact that he owned horses of considerable value, and to this day figures in marble of horses dedicated by him in commemoration of his victories at Olympia are to be seen in the local museum of Delphi.

Almost every year attempts are made by wealthy Americans and others to purchase some of these figures, but down to the present such attempts have proved of no avail.

Plato, again, has much to say upon the horse in its relation to the history of his epoch. Thus in one place he writes: "We must mount our children on horses in their earliest youth, and take them on horseback to see war, in order that they may learn to ride; the horses must not be spirited or warlike, but the most tractable and yet the swiftest that can be had; in this way they will get an excellent view of what is hereafter to be their business; and if there is danger they have only to follow their elder leaders and escape."

48

Agrigentum—until 405 B.C., when it was destroyed by the Carthaginians—was famous for its horses. It is said that on one occasion, when one of the best-known citizens, Exænetus, won the principal chariot race at Olympus, the entire population came forth to meet him, and that he was preceded into the city by 300 chariots drawn by pairs of white horses. Indeed some of the most gorgeous monuments ever erected to the memory of famous race horses were those raised in this city during the period of its splendour.

1. THE EMPEROR TRAJAN. SHOWING ROMAN STYLE OF RIDING
2. THE EMPEROR THEODOSIUS. SHOWING SADDLE
3. A PARTHIAN HORSEMAN. SHOWING PARTHIAN STYLE OF RIDING BAREBACK
4. SARMATHIAN HORSE AND WARRIOR. MEANT TO REPRESENT HORSE AND RIDER IN ARMOUR MADE OF PLATES OF BONE OR OF HORSE-HOOF

We have it on good authority that, some centuries before Christ, the Persian men of rank deemed it derogatory to be seen on foot, and that they habitually rode on horseback. Yet in common with the people of many other races they were addicted to immolating horses on festival days, while the practices in which they indulged upon these occasions are said to have been barbarous in the extreme.

In almost every age white horses in particular would seem to have been used for sacrificial purposes. The Persians sacrificed bulls as well as horses, a bull and a horse being sometimes bound together and then immolated. Arrian mentions that one horse at least was sacrificed to Cyrus every month, the ceremony being usually performed at Pasargadea, close to the famous tomb. Here again white horses were used for the sacrifices, for among the Persians in particular the white horse was for many centuries deemed sacred and pronounced "beloved of the gods."

One of the descriptions that probably gives a true account of a triumphal march in the third century B.C. is that of Herodotus, where he describes the procession of Xerxes. The following order, he tells us, was observed.

There came first 1000 carefully selected horsemen, then 1000 carefully selected spearsmen, then ten sacred Nisæan horses "splendidly caparisoned." These horses were called Nisæan, we are incidentally told, because they were especially reared on the plains of Nisæa, in Media, at that period famous for its great horses.

Next came the sacred car of Zeus, drawn by eight white horses "followed by charioteers on foot holding their bridles, for no mortal was allowed to mount the seat." Xerxes himself brought up the train, usually in a chariot drawn by Nisæan horses, with his charioteer beside him.

The people of almost every nation of whom we have authentic records would appear to have been addicted in the centuries before Christ to the atrocious practice of sacrificing live horses to their gods. Particulars of the weird rites observed in connection with these sacrifices are for the most part too revolting to be described here, but one practice observed by the Scythians cannot well be passed unnoticed.

This people inhabited chiefly the treeless steppes of Asia, and is known to have sacrificed animals of many kinds, but horses most of all, and usually white or dun horses.

Thus we are told that when a Scythian king died, his favourite horse, his favourite concubine, and several important members of his establishment, preferably his cook and his cupbearer, were buried with him. When a year had passed, a further ceremony took place.

This consisted in the execution, generally by strangulation, of some fifty of the strongest, handsomest and generally most desirable young men—probably young men who had belonged to his suite—and in the strangulation also of an equal number of the best horses that had belonged to him.

Then, without delay, the bodies of men and horses were disembowelled, next they were stuffed with chaff or straw, and finally when the horses, supplied each with a bit and bridle, had been set up in a circle round the tomb of the deceased monarch, the bodies of the slaughtered men were set astride them.

And there the ghastly squadron remained until it fell away to dust.

That the literary records in which these gruesome details

are to be found are accurate, has to some extent been proved by discoveries made from time to time—as for instance at the opening of the great tumuli in Russia about half-a-century ago.

Indeed during the thirteenth century A.D. ceremonies equally revolting are known to have been performed regularly among the Tartars, while at the funeral of Frederic Casimir, Commander of Lorraine, in 1781, a horse was killed, and then buried with its master, and at even so recent a date as the funeral of Li Hung Chang a horse and chariot made of paper were, according to the newspaper reports, burned at the grave-side—probably a last survival of some weird rite of a sacrificial nature observed formerly in China and Japan.

Another race known to have immolated live horses, especially white horses, was the Veneti. This people lived at the head of the Adriatic, and their name survives to this day in "Venice."

The sacrifice of white horses was common too amongst the Scandinavian and the Teutonic races, and formed part of their religion. The Sicilian Greeks, again, are said to have set a high value upon white horses, and to have sacrificed them under the impression that by doing so they afforded additional gratification to their gods.

It would appear, indeed, that in all ages white animals were looked upon as sacred in a sense, for in parts of India the white elephant is deemed sacred to this day, and in parts of Persia the white ass. Then, in the fifth century B.C., the nomad Scythians, whose territories lay chiefly to the north of the River Don, owned immense herds of horses. These they used principally for food, while the milk of the mares they drank and made domestic use of in other ways, a practice long in vogue among the Turko-Tartaric tribes of

Central Asia, and said to be still in vogue with them in remote regions.

Bearing upon early Persia is rather a well-known story that on the death of the famous Smerdis the seven princes who were his possible successors agreed to confer the throne upon the owner of the horse that should be the first to neigh when they all met on the following day. The groom of Prince Darius having been told of this, had recourse to a clever ruse, for on that same evening he led his master's horse to the exact spot where the horses were all to meet on the day following, and there showed the horse a mare. Upon arriving at this spot next day the horse, as we are told, "neighed furiously," so that Darius won his kingdom!

We know that Hiero, King of Syracuse, who flourished towards the end of the third and during the beginning of the second century, B.C., won the great Olympic crown with his good horse Phrenicus. In simple language Tacitus describes how the people of Thurii—the city built on the ruins of Sybaris about the year 443 B.C.—first taught horse racing to the Romans.

Although towards the end of the second century B.C., bareback riding was still quite common, a covering of some sort for the horse's back was becoming much more popular among the Greeks despite the adherence to bareback riding by the jockeys at the principal festivals. Atiphanes, the "gentle humourist," whose plays were performed in public for the first time towards the close of the second century B.C., alludes to "coverlets for a horse," this being probably one of the first references we have to saddles among the early Greeks.

And now we come to Xenophon, one of the most finished of horsemen among the ancient Greeks, and apparently a true lover of horses. With the exception of an individual named Simo, or Simon, who wrote before Xenophon's time, there had not existed a man with deep and practical knowledge of horses or horsemanship, and the care of horses, who was able to write lucidly upon these subjects until Xenophon wrote with so much success his own exhaustive work.

Xenophon speaks of Simo—who, according to Suidas, was by birth an Athenian—on more than one occasion. Xenophon, however, did not hold Simo in high esteem, as we may gather from the former's tone of condescension when he states that though Simo wrote with some knowledge of horses, yet that he entertained an exalted opinion of himself that was unpardonable.

A PORTION OF THE PARTHENON FRIEZE, EXECUTED BY PHIDIAS
ABOUT THE YEAR 440 B.C.

The truth of that statement is borne out by the evidence we have that when, on a famous occasion, Simo presented the brazen horse to the temple of the Eleusinian Ceres, at Athens, he had the effrontery to engrave upon the pedestal his own works!

Though when expressing opinions upon the points of a horse the ancient Greeks differed rather widely in their views, yet most of the rules laid down by Xenophon are as applicable to-day as they were some three and twenty centuries ago.

We read, for instance, that "the neck of the horse, as it proceeds from the chest, should not fall forward, like that of a boar, but should grow upward, like that of a cock, and should have an easy motion at the parts about the arch." That the advice was not overlooked, even by early artists, can be accurately conjectured if the Parthenon frieze be inspected, for there almost every horse shown has a neck "like that of a cock." Xenophon then proceeds:

"If a horse has the thighs under the tail broad and not distorted, he will set his hind legs well apart, and will by that means have a firmer and quicker step, a better seat for a rider, and be better in every respect. We may see," he continues, "a proof of this in men, who when they wish to take up anything from the ground do try to raise it by setting their legs apart rather than by bringing them together."

These remarks are sensible, yet probably there are few modern horsemen ready to admit that a horse's hoof should be high and hollow, and the frog kept up from the ground "as well before as behind," which was Xenophon's opinion. Then in his time saddles and stirrups had not, apparently, been thought of, for we read that when first introduced they were looked upon with scorn, all who used them being laughed at and deemed to take rank among what we should call in these days "muffs."

As already noted, Xenophon had something to say upon bits and bitting, and he describes at length the advantages of the jointed over the rigid bit. Also he alludes to the custom of wearing spurs, and describes incidentally the construction of the prick spurs then in vogue.

In this connection it is interesting to note that a bit was discovered in the Acropolis of Athens some twenty years ago, which, so it is said, dates back to the early Persian wars of 490-479 B.C.

Certain modern writers of books upon subjects more or less historical speak of horse doctors. Some twenty-three centuries ago, however, even the acknowledged experts upon horses and horse breeding would seem to have possessed only crude anatomical knowledge of the animal, some of the advice they tendered in cases of illness amongst horses being grotesque.

Equally it is evident that professional horse breakers and trainers, also professional riding masters, were known in Greece in Xenophon's day, and possibly before his time.

There is something rather delightful about Xenophon's ingenuousness when he tells us quite seriously that "a horse that has no longer the marks in his teeth, neither rejoices the buyer with hope, nor is easy to be exchanged"! He speaks too with emphasis when assuring us that when carefully examining a horse with a view to purchase we ought to pay most attention to the hoofs—advice to some extent discounted by remarks he makes a few lines further on.

"To sum up all in a few words," he says elsewhere, "whatever horse has good feet, is mild-tempered, sufficiently swift, and able to endure fatigue, and is in the highest degree obedient, will probably give least trouble to his rider and contribute most to his safety in military occupations. But horses that from sluggishness require a great deal of driving, or, from excess of mettle, much coaxing and care, afford plenty of employment to the rider, as well as much apprehension in time of danger."

The ancients evidently had a rooted antipathy to adopting any kind of contrivance calculated to afford protection for their horses' hoofs. Upon several occasions attempts were made to introduce metal horseshoes, but in vain. The device most resembling a horseshoe, that they were willing to consider and of which we have a trustworthy description, was a covering not unlike a sandal made of reeds, or, in rare instances, of leather. In reality it resembled a boot rather than a horseshoe, but it was used only where the ground was very rough or exceptionally hard.

In parts of Japan boots of this kind, made of straw, are worn to this day. Berenger speaks of a horseshoe said to have been in use in the time of Childeric, whose date was 481, A.D., and most likely it was one of the first horseshoes, properly so called, of which any record is extant.

If the figure of it preserved in Montfaucon's "Antiquities" is to be relied upon for accuracy, then it somewhat resembled the shoe in use to-day.

It seems clear that Xenophon was not an advocate for docking horses' tails, at any rate to the exaggerated extent we so often see them docked to-day, also that he was not partial to the hogged mane, for in speaking of the horse's forelocks, "while these hairs," he avers, "though of good length, do not prevent the horse from seeing, they brush away from his eyes whatever annoys them. Therefore we may suppose that the gods gave such hairs to the horse instead of the long ears which they have given to asses and mules to be a protection to the eyes."

―――――――――

A question sometimes set when the subject of early horsemanship is under discussion is: How used the ancients to mount, seeing that they placed at best only cloths on their horses' backs, and that they had not stirrups?

Historical records contain information upon the point, and we read that in the centuries before Christ horses were mounted apparently in three ways—by the rider's vaulting without assistance on to the back; by his vaulting or mounting with the aid of a pole; by his making the horse crouch.

There was a fourth way, but for an obvious reason it was less often resorted to. This was by making a slave bend his back, or kneel on all fours, and by then stepping upon him —using him as a mounting-block, in short. The last-named method was common in Persia, where Sapor, when he had conquered the Emperor Valerian, forced him thus to debase himself to show his complete subjection.

I believe I am right in saying that the soldiery used sometimes to mount with the aid of a spear. Xenophon, in his seventh chapter, instructs the horseman to mount "by catching hold of the mane, about the ears," a feat surely impossible to perform save when mounting a pony.

In the illustration of a Sarmatian on horseback, facing page 33, both a man and horse are shown in armour made of horse-hoof cut into little plates, which, Pausanias tells us in his Attics, were sewn together with the sinews of oxen and horses. Sometimes bone was used in place of horse-hoof, but iron never, there being no iron mines in the country, to the knowledge of the Sarmatians. The soldier shown holding up his horse's leg, in the illustration facing page 45, presumably is about to tie on one of the "stockings" used in place of shoes; and on the same plate a soldier is about to mount on the off (right) side.

ROMAN SOLDIER ABOUT TO ADJUST "STOCKING" USED IN PLACE OF SHOES

ROMAN SOLDIER ABOUT TO MOUNT ON OFF SIDE

A MAURITANIAN HORSEMAN. SHOWING HOW THE MAURITANIANS

60

AND HUMIDIANS RODE WITHOUT SADDLE OR BRIDLE

CHAPTER III

IN spite of the derisive remarks often uttered concerning Xenophon's advice to young riders, and his advice on horsemanship in general and the care of horses, there is much sound sense in plenty of the hints he gave to the Greek riders of three hundred years before Christ, while many of the rules he laid down are as applicable to-day as they probably were then.

His advice on the vexed question of bits and bitting, to take but a single example, is very sound, while his strong objection to allowing horses' legs to be washed frequently is shared by plenty of horse owners at the present time.

Then, the old Athenian apparently disapproved of or disliked what we have come to call the "American" seat on a horse, for he declares that the legs of a man mounted should be almost straight, the body upright and supple.

Attempts have repeatedly been made to trace the life of Xenophon prior to the time when, in 401 B.C., he first joined the army of Cyrus, but in vain. He is, however, known to have been a close friend of Socrates from a very early age, and probably when he wrote the "Anabasis" he was a little over thirty. But when he died, about the year 355 B.C., he was quite an old man.

Historians are almost unanimous in declaring that at Marathon, in 490 B.C., the Athenians were without cavalry, though by that time many of the wealthy citizens undoubtedly owned horses, some of which they most likely used for racing. When, however, the Athenians came to realise what an amount of execution could be done, and to see the execution that was done by the Persians, with the help of cavalry, they set to work to organise in Athens, as quickly as possible, a powerful body of mounted warriors.

How formidable that cavalry later on proved itself to be is well known to all classical scholars, and the more surprising it therefore is that the Greek cavalry should not afterwards have risen to the level of that organised by Macedonians. Indeed, according to more than one historian, the Greek cavalry was employed chiefly to harass an enemy when marching, or to pursue a vanquished and retreating regiment, while one writer at least maintains that the Greek cavalry at best never approached within javelin range of an enemy's line of battle during an attack.

The cost of horses at about this time varied almost as widely as it does now. Thus it was not unusual to pay three minæ, the equivalent of about fifteen guineas, for quite a common hack—an extraordinarily high price when we bear in mind the purchasing value of money in those days—while for trained war horses, or for race horses, any sum from ten minæ upward was paid frequently.

Xenophon is known to have given approximately eleven minæ for a little war horse that, so far as one can ascertain, did not afterwards fulfil expectations, so perhaps it is hardly astonishing to read that some years later the terms "horse owner" and "spendthrift" came to be deemed more or less synonymous.

A list drawn up at about this time of the principal defects to be guarded against when inspecting a horse with a view to purchase is interesting, inasmuch as the points looked upon as faults three and twenty centuries ago are with only a few exceptions deemed to be egregious defects to-day.

The following is the list that was drawn up, so it is alleged, by Pollux:

Hoofs with thin horn (sic); hoofs full, fat, soft and flat—or, as Xenophon termed them, "low-lying"; heavy fetlocks; shanks with varicose veins; flabby thighs; hollow shoulder-blades; projecting neck; bald mane; narrow chest; fat and heavy head; large ears; converging nostrils; sunken eyes; thin and meagre sides; sharp back-bone; rough haunches; thin buttocks; stiff legs, stiff knees.

Though among the horses of the ancient Greeks the hogged mane must at one time have been seen often enough, there does not appear to be in the works of the early writers any direct allusion to the hogging of horses as a regular practice.

Probably if the custom did exist it was on the wane by the time Xenophon began to write. There is evidence to show that in ancient Greece the horses at about this period were rather smaller than those of most other countries of which we have authentic records, a characteristic still noticeable amongst the horses in several parts of modern Greece.

The Greeks almost always used entire horses for all purposes. Even in war they did not employ geldings, a custom that has given rise to the belief that in the centuries before Christ all horses, with the exception of the Libyan steeds, were far more savage than the horses of to-day.

Emphatically we have no reason to suppose that the Greeks made friends and companions of their horses as the Arab race is known to do or to have done, though the fable of Achilles' love for his horse named Xanthus makes a pretty enough story. On the other hand, it is quite possible that Xenophon may have been fond of horses not merely because of the amusement they afforded him or the pleasure he derived from riding and hunting.

For the rest the Greeks, in common with the people of most of the warlike nations in those early days, enjoyed possessing horses mainly because they served to enhance life's pleasure, and were of practical use in war.

Certainly it may be said of Xenophon that he did not preach the doctrine of kindness to horses without himself practising it thoroughly, also that he was ever ready to rebuke severely all who ill-treated their own horses or his.

Apparently the Greeks of about this era did not keep what we should term to-day pleasure horses, though they affected pleasure horses in the sense that they kept race horses. With the death of Xenophon we lose touch, to some extent, with the progress of the horse in history, but the thread is taken up again in the Roman period when Varro, writing in 37 B.C., furnishes certain details that are of interest, Virgil adding to them a little later in his "Georgics."

After that we find instructive comment in the writings of Calpurnius and Columella in the first century A.D.; in those of Oppian and Nemesian in the third century; and in those of Apsyrtus, Pelagonius and Palladius in the fourth century.

━━━━━━━━

When all is said, Xenophon's information most likely is by far the most trustworthy of any that has been handed down to us, in the same way that his descriptions certainly are the most accurate. Only a few fragments of the book by Simo, written probably about the year 460 B.C., remain; yet even those fragments contain peculiar statements.

Thus in addition to insinuating that Thessaly was the only region famous for horses in the centuries before Christ —an assertion indirectly gainsaid by Xenophon—he didactically remarks that the colour of a horse ought not to be taken into consideration when the animal's qualities are being summed up, a statement that the majority of the early writers openly repudiated, and that, as most of us know, is in every country deemed devoid of truth at the present day.

Though particulars are difficult to obtain, there is reason to believe that the horse named after the Thracian river, Strymon—owing to its having been bred in that vicinity— and that was immolated by Xerxes before his invasion of Greece, was, as usual, a white horse.

By exactly what route horses were introduced into Greece has not been ascertained for certain, but the fact that fossilised remains of horses have not been found in Greece as they have been in many other countries leads to the belief that the horse was not indigenous to the country.

From a very remote period, however, we find horses represented on vase paintings; and from these paintings too we are able practically to prove that the Greeks had not rowels in their primitive spurs, but that the spur consisted of a short goad attached to the heel of the boot by means of a strap passing over the instep and another that passed under the sole, almost as the modern hunting spur is strapped on. Spurs of this kind have been discovered in Olympia, also in Magna Græcia, and elsewhere.

With regard to the Greek bits and bridles of a later date,

the former apparently had no leverage—certainly they had no curb chain—while the pattern of the bridle seems to have remained unaltered.

As we come nearer still to the time of Christ, we find the young men of Athens growing fonder and fonder of horse racing and taking more pains and spending much time and money in their attempts to improve the breed of horses. And though the soil of Attica was by no means adapted for purposes of horse rearing, it must in justice be said that their attempts met with reward.

Thus it happened that about this time—that is to say towards the close of the third or the beginning of the second century—the comic poet, Aristophanes, who died in 380 B.C., began to inveigh against the increasing popularity of horse racing, and against the spread of gambling consequent thereon.

In his immortal comedy of *The Clouds*, it will be remembered, he portrays a typical young spendthrift, Pheidippes, and an equally typical indignant father, Strepsiades, both of whom would serve well as latter-day types of men of the same stamp.

The son, when the comedy opens, has lost heavily on the turf and incurred the displeasure, not to say roused the indignation, of his father, in addition to burdening the old man heavily with his gambling debts. Presently the son is sued by Pasion, a characteristic usurer of that period, for the recovery of the entire sum of twelve minæ.

"For what with debts and duns and stablekeepers' bills," Strepsiades exclaims in exasperation in the opening lines, addressing his son Pheidippes, who lies asleep before him — "what with debts and duns and stablekeepers' bills which this fine spark heaps on my back, I lie awake the whilst: and what cares he but to coil up his locks, ride, drive his horses, dream of them all night...." And so on.

This gives us, to start with, an idea of the degree of popularity that horse racing had attained in Greece at about this time, for Pheidippes is meant to be a character drawn from life and typical of the young punters of the period.

Later we learn that the money for which the father is being sued had, in the first instance, been borrowed to pay for a "starling-coloured horse"—whatever kind of weird creature that may have been. Possibly "fleabitten" is intended, for the geographer, Strabo, speaks of "the starling-coloured horses of the Parthians" and of the people of Northern Spain, and it is known that plenty of those horses were of the colour that we should term to-day "fleabitten."

———————————

Aristotle is the next to enlighten us to some extent upon the growing fondness of the Greeks for horses, especially for race horses and war horses. He tells us too that about the average span the horses in his time—the middle of the second century B.C., 384 to 322—lived was eighteen to twenty years, though a few were said to have reached five and twenty, and even thirty, and a very few indeed to have died at fifty.

Whether the custom that then prevailed of feeding horses mostly on barley proved beneficial or the reverse in the long run we are not told. Finally we come to Alexander the Great and his renowned Bucephalus, a horse bred, as we are told, by Philoneicus of Pharsalus, a Thessalian.

Bucephalus, or rather Bucephal*os*, means ox head, or bull head, from which we may conclude that whatever good points Bucephalus may have had—and without doubt he had many—he certainly had not the fine head of a modern hunter or the tapering muzzle of the thoroughbred that nowadays we so much admire.

It has been stated that Bucephalus derived his name from a mark on the left shoulder in the form more or less of a bull's head. As we know, however, that many years before Alexander's Bucephalus was foaled there existed a type of Thessalian horse upon which the same name had been bestowed, the conjecture is probably a false one.

How great the fame of Bucephalus was may be gathered from the fact that of all the horses possessed by the ancient Greeks down to this date he alone is the animal over which they thoroughly "enthuse." From what we are told in the writings of Aristotle, indeed, and of later historians, Bucephalus must have been quite a tall horse, well shaped, coal-black, with a good shoulder and small ears. Also he had a white star in the middle of his forehead, a mark characteristic of certain Libyan breeds of old.

ALEXANDER THE GREAT ON HORSEBACK, ABOUT 338 B.C. THE
FIGURE IS BELIEVED TO REPRESENT BUCEPHALUS
From a bronze in the British Museum

An unknown writer in the "Geoponics" avers that in the centuries just before Christ many of the best horses had eyes of different colour—what we sometimes term a wall eye, and Americans a China eye—and from his own deductions he concludes that Bucephalus probably had eyes that did not match. There does not, however, appear to be direct evidence that this was so.

Plutarch sets the price paid for Bucephalus by Alexander's father, King Philip, at thirteen talents, while Pliny is of opinion that the price was higher still—namely, sixteen talents.

Now the sum that to-day would be the equivalent of thirteen talents is approximately £3500, and when we bear in mind the prices that in the second century frequently were paid even for the best horses obtainable, and recollect, in addition, that at the time King Philip bought Bucephalus the horse was probably aged—some writers aver that he must have been quite fourteen when Philip bought him—it is not possible to reconcile the statement that a fancy price in any way approaching the sum named could have been paid.

The story of the trial and subsequent purchase of Bucephalus is both pretty and picturesque. More, it would appear to be true in almost every detail. According to Plutarch, whose account probably is the most trustworthy, the horse was first brought before King Philip to be given a public trial, when, to the discomfiture of its owner, it showed itself to be apparently "a fierce and unmanageable beast that would neither allow anybody to mount him, nor obey any of Philip's attendants, but reared and plunged against them all, so that the king in a rage bade them take him away for an utterly wild and unbroken brute."

At this juncture it was that Alexander—at the time a boy of twelve, and Aristotle not yet his tutor—came upon the scene. We are told that he "leapt suddenly forward and in an access of indignation cried out before the king and everybody assembled that the men attempting to ride the horse were 'clumsy clowns,'" adding, with the self-assurance of precocious boyhood, that "if they were not careful they would spoil the horse entirely."

Philip at first paid no attention to his son's outburst, deeming it to be childish spleen, but upon the lad's refusing to be quieted he turned to him, suddenly nettled, and demanded in a sharp tone how he dare be so insolent as to criticise his elders. In no way abashed, Alexander retorted that in this instance he certainly did know much better than his elders, and that if his father would allow him he would prove it by himself mounting the horse at once and riding it round the ring.

"And what will you forfeit for your rashness if you are thrown off?" the king inquired, not troubling to conceal his anger.

To which young Alexander retorted with much spirit:

"The price of the horse, by Zeus!"

It is hardly likely that Alexander, rash though he undoubtedly was, would have said this if the price at which Bucephalus was valued amounted to a sum in talents equivalent to thousands of pounds, for King Philip though a just ruler was a stern father, and Alexander must have known that his father would extort the forfeit should he fail to ride the horse.

The lad's reply, we are told, was received with shouts of laughter. This public expression of ridicule it may have been that set the boy upon his mettle, for without further parley he ran out into the arena, ordered his father's attendants aside, and then, grasping the reins, began to pat the horse's neck and "soothe him with soft words."

For the boy had observed what apparently nobody else had noticed—namely, that the horse grew restive at the sight of its own shadow. Without waiting, therefore, he turned the horse to face the sun, then at once "sprang up and bestrode him unharmed." Next, gradually and very gently, and using neither whip nor spur, he made Bucephalus move round and round in a circle until the animal no longer feared its shadow and then when it had, as we are told, "given up all threatening behaviour, and was only hot for the course," he gave the horse its head, "urging him onward by raising his voice and using his heel."

At the sight of this fine display of horse breaking and

horsemanship the spectators, now somewhat abashed at the haste they had been in to jeer, grew silent. But not for long. Presently, as Alexander came galloping back, "full of just pride and pleasure," the assembled multitude, including the king's attendants, "of one accord raised a great cheer, lifting up their hands from pure joy."

Philip himself must have been of an emotional nature, for we read that "he said nothing, but wept silently from pure joy."

Possibly the lad too suffered from "pure joy" at that moment, for upon his dismounting his father advanced with the remark that Macedonia was "not big enough for such a son," that he "must go look for a kingdom to match him."

Which shows that even in the centuries before Christ there was truth in the popular platitude that nothing succeeds like success!

Then and there Bucephalus was bought for Alexander, and from that time until its death, from wounds received in a battle fought against the Indian king, Porus, the horse remained Alexander's favourite charger and companion.

A remarkable peculiarity about this animal was that though subsequently it came to allow the grooms to ride it bareback, yet when it had on one of the cloths that at that period did duty for a saddle it would allow only Alexander to mount it. As one writer neatly says: "When others tried to mount the horse with the cloth on they invariably had to take to their heels to save themselves from his." It is further recorded that when Alexander wished to mount, Bucephalus would crouch of its own accord to enable its master to get on more easily.

Alexander took Bucephalus with him on his famous

expeditions into the East, and on one occasion, in Hyrcania, the horse was stolen. The king "thereupon became terrible to see, so great was his rage." At once an edict was issued that unless the horse were returned to him without delay he would "carry fire and sword throughout the country—north and south, east and west, sparing neither men nor women, nor, if need be, even the smallest children."

A chronicler of the period, commenting upon this, drily observes that when Alexander's determination became known, "the horse was returned in a hurry!"

"Thus," remarks Arrian, the great historian, "the horse must have been as dear to Alexander as Alexander was terrible to the barbarians." As he here employs the word "barbarian" in its offensive signification he evidently despised the people of Hyrcania because they had sense enough to return the stolen horse instead of waiting with their kith and kin to be slain or tortured!

In the descriptions of almost all the great victories won by Alexander the Great, allusion is made to his favourite steed. We are told by Gellius that in the battle that practically witnessed the death of Bucephalus the king had pressed forward recklessly into the thick of the fight, and apparently right into the enemy's lines, and had thus become "the mark for every spear"—a statement which, if literally true, points to an enemy made up of singularly inept marksmen.

"More than one spear," he goes on, "was buried in the neck and flanks of the horse, but, though at the point of death, and almost drained of blood, he succeeded with a bold dash in carrying the king from the very midst of the foe, and then fell, breathing his last tranquilly now that he knew his master was safe, and as comforted by the knowledge as if he had had the feelings of a human being."

There is something about the concluding sentence that leads to the belief that Gellius must have been either remarkably imaginative, or else of a more romantic nature than the majority of his contemporaries have given him credit for being. The last line in particular is very precious. After reading it can one feel astonished at Alexander's enthusiasm having carried him to the length of causing him to build a city to the memory of the noble steed, a city to which he gave the name Bucephala?

The handsome bronze discovered in Herculaneum is popularly supposed to represent the figures of Alexander and Bucephalus. The work probably of Lysippus—whom Alexander himself ordered to produce a scene representing a fight during the great battle of Granicus—it is extremely interesting.

A pleasing anecdote told of Alexander and Bucephalus, and more likely to be true than are the majority of the tales that are related of this horse and its owner, is to the effect that upon one occasion the king went to inspect a portrait of himself mounted on his favourite charger, that the distinguished painter, Apelles, had just completed.

Nettled at Alexander's scant praise of his work—for we are told the picture was so lifelike that even Bucephalus neighed when first he saw it—Apelles turned to the king with the rebuke:

"I fear me, your Majesty, that your horse is a better judge of painting than his noble master."

What retort the king made is not recorded, but the story recalls one of a similar nature related of the famous artist, Pauson, who when ordered to produce a picture of a horse rolling on its back, sent to his patron a picture of a horse galloping madly through a cloud of dust.

In a great rage the patron sent for Pauson, and, upon his arrival, "began to storm and rave," at the same time demanding to know what had made him commit a blunder so egregious. Without replying, Pauson walked up to the picture and turned it upside down, when, to the vast amusement of the hitherto irate patron, there appeared a perfect picture of a horse rolling on its back on a dusty plain.

Of the famous artist, Micon, it is related that he once incurred the criticism of the rider, Simon, who, upon looking at one of his pictures, remarked drily that never in his life before had he seen a horse that had eyelashes on its lower lids!

It seems certain that in the centuries before Christ the steeds bred in Thessaly were among the most highly prized, though the horses of several other breeds—such, for instance, as the Argive, the Arcadian, the Epidaurian and the Arcananian—possessed great courage and exceptional power of endurance.

PERSIANS FIGHTING WITH ELEPHANTS AGAINST THE ROMANS,
ABOUT THE TIME OF PYRRHUS, 280 B.C.
This picture has been wrongly attributed to Raphael

In the very early times Thessalian horses were used largely for charioteering. Allusion is made repeatedly in the classics to these Thessalian animals, stress being laid upon their symmetry, or what to-day we should term their make and shape. The mythical mares of King Diomed of Thrace, the tyrant whose grim humour, we are told, led him to feed his horses on the strangers who visited his kingdom, were alleged to be of the breed of Thessaly, a statement made indirectly in the description of Hercules' conquest of the tyrant and his subsequent "casting of the tyrant's quivering carcass to his own horses to be devoured."

Spenser alludes to this incident in the fifth book of his "Faerie Queene," in the following lines:—

77

"Like to the Thracian tyrant who, they say,
Unto his horses gave his guests for meat,
Till he himself was made their greedy prey,
And torn to pieces by Alcides great."

Other mythical horses of the Thessalian breed were those of Achilles, of Rhesus, and of Orestes in Sophocles' stirring description of the race in *Electra*.

It seems safe to say that until about the fourth century B.C. the Romans also did not use saddles, at least saddles with trees. That somewhere about this period, however, they began to adopt what we should call to-day saddlecloths, and that these were kept in place by a strap or bandage in the nature of a girth that passed beneath the belly, appears to be certain.

For some unknown reason this girth is more often than not omitted on the works of art that represent horses of that period. Some of the animals of the Parthenon frieze lead us to believe that on occasions horses were still made to crouch when about to be mounted, though it is not probable they crouched voluntarily, as Bucephalus did. From impressions on the Parthenon frieze we may also conclude that the mounting block was not unknown in the centuries before Christ.

A good idea of the exact stamp of horse harnessed to the war chariots of those centuries may be obtained by inspecting the bronze horse of the quadriga from the Mausoleum at Halicarnassus, the date of the Mausoleum being 331-341 B.C.—the building took ten years to erect. This bronze is to be seen in the British Museum.

Hannibal's must have been the army the best provided with cavalry down to the year 218 B.C., for in that year Hannibal advanced into Italy with no less than 90,000 foot and some 12,000 horse, many of the latter being native horses mounted by Numidians who persisted still in scorning to use either saddle or bridle, though the cavalry division, which consisted of Spaniards, employed bridles of an elaborate pattern.

How wholly superior Hannibal's cavalry proved to be to the Gallic horsemen placed by Scipio in the front line of his javelin throwers is well known to students of history. Indeed it was said that Hannibal's horsemen were superior even to the Italian and the Roman cavalry, which was high praise.

——————

Probably from about the year 200 B.C., possibly from an even earlier period, the Romans used spurs, apparently the common prick spurs which remained in vogue until towards the middle of the thirteenth century A.D. Some half-a-century later, or about the year 150 B.C., there were issued in succession a series of Gaulish silver coins, the majority of which bore upon one side the impression of a horseman, though comparatively few showed the chariot at one time so generally represented on coins.

This leads naturally to the inference that the popularity of the chariot was already waning. Chariots, however, continued to appear upon the gold coins made in imitation of the gold stater of Philip II. of Macedon, coins that bore on the face Apollo's head, on the reverse a two-horse chariot.

Exceptionally fine horses, probably with Liberian blood in them, must have been owned by the Iberians and Celtiberians at about the period the Stoic philosopher Posidonius was travelling in Western Europe, and when he incidentally visited Spain—about the year 90 B.C.

Posidonius himself remarks that the cavalry of the Iberians was trained to travel over mountains, adding that these horses too would crouch when told to, in order that their riders might mount or dismount with greater ease.

A method to which this cavalry sometimes had recourse consisted in their mounting two men on one animal. Then, in the heat of action, one of the men would fight on foot, the other remaining by to defend him if hard pressed. The same philosopher tells us that the horses of the Parthians and Celtiberians "indeed were superior to all other breeds in fleetness and endurance."

CHAPTER IV

Virgil on the points of a horse—Cæsar's invasion—Abolition of war chariots
—Precursor of the horseshoe—Nero's 2000 mules shod with silver; Poppæa's
shod with gold—The Ossianic and Cuchulainn epic cycles; Cuchulainn's
horses—The Iceni on Newmarket Heath; early horse racing in Britain—
Horses immolated by the Romans; white horses as prognosticators—
Caligula's horse, Incitatus; Celer, the horse of Verus; the horse of Belisarius

VIRGIL, whose famous "Georgics" was published about the year 29 B.C., incidentally shows how close the connection was that in his time existed between men and their horses— that is, in so far as the former would probably have gained comparatively few victories and made but little headway in civilisation had they not been materially helped by "man's friend and ally, the horse."

According to Virgil, in the years just before Christ the colour least liked in horses intended for work was white. "Yellow" also was objected to, the prevalent belief being that white or dun horses must *ipso facto* be of weak constitution. White markings were not disliked, however, and we read that Virgil's Roman youth rode "a Thracian steed of two colours," it had a white fore foot and a forehead with a white patch. The charger ridden by Turnus was also a Thracian horse, with markings somewhat similar.

The following description in the third book of Virgil's "Georgics" gives us most likely an approximate idea of some points that were looked for in a good horse in the last century B.C.:—

"Choose with like care the courser's generous breed,
And from his birth prepare the parent steed.
His colour mark, select the glossy bay,
And to the white or dun prefer the grey.
As yet a colt he stalks with lofty pace,
And balances his limbs with flexile grace:
First leads the way, the threatening torrent braves,
And dares the unknown arch that spans the waves.
Light on his airy crest his slender head,
His belly short, his loins luxuriant spread:
Muscle on muscle knots his brawny breast,
No fear alarms him, nor vain shouts molest.
But at the clash of arms, his ear afar
Drinks the deep sound, and vibrates to the war:
Flames from each nostril roll in gathered stream,
His quivering limbs with restless motion gleam,
O'er his right shoulder, floating full and fair,
Sweeps his thick mane, and spreads its pomp of hair:
Swift works his double spine, and earth around
Rings to his solid hoof that wears the ground."

Though chariots were still in use among the Belgic tribes who inhabited the south-eastern portion of the island when, in 55 B.C., Cæsar invaded Britain, cavalry must have been coming into vogue with them, for we read that "no sooner were these tribes warned to be prepared for Cæsar's contemplated invasion than they sent forward cavalry and charioteers, which formed their chief arm in warfare."

The people of North Britain, however, still paid but little attention to the advice of the more intelligent among their chiefs that cavalry ought to be adopted and chariots entirely discarded, the principle of ultra-conservatism which remains one of the most marked characteristics of the British nation at the present day being apparently in force even in Cæsar's time.

By this period the Gauls, as Cæsar soon found out, had become a nation composed almost wholly of knights. Yet whether the aboriginal horse of the first yeomanry of Kent that met Cæsar upon his landing belonged to the breed believed to have been imported by the Celts or Germans, or whether they were descendants of the horses known to have been largely bred when Hannibal's warlike expeditions into Spain, Gaul and Italy were over, is not known.

Of interest it is to be told that the men who invaded this country under the banner of the White Horse greatly valued the particular breed of horses they found here, and that in consequence their descendants in later centuries cut upon the chalk cliffs of the Berkshire downs near Ilsley and Wantage the rough figures of horses that remain there to this day.

We have it on the authority of several of the most trustworthy of our early historians that by about the end of the third century B.C., at latest, the Gauls of northern Italy had become a race of horsemen; that by about the middle of the second century B.C. the majority of the Transalpine Gauls had done the same; and that by Cæsar's time even the Belgic tribes of the Continent had practically abandoned the war chariot that the Romans had deemed so helpful.

Apparently the horses employed by the Roman warriors were of a better stamp than those which belonged to the Gauls of Northern Italy.

It is well known that Cæsar's opinion of the value of chariots in war was, to say the least, rather inflated. His description of the action of war chariots during an engagement is of itself almost sufficient to prove this.

"At the first onset," he writes, "they [the warriors] drove the cars in all directions, hurled their javelins, and by the din and clatter of horses and wheels commonly threw the ranks of the enemy into disorder.

83

"Then, making their way amongst the squadrons of the enemy's cavalry, they leaped down from the chariots and fought on foot.

"Little by little the charioteers withdrew out of the fight and placed their chariots in such a way that if they were hard pressed by the enemy they could readily retreat to their own side.

"Thus in battle they afforded the mobility of cavalry, and the steadiness of infantry.

"Daily practice enabled them to pull up their horses when in full speed on a slope or steep declivity, to check or turn them in a narrow space, to run out on the pole and stand on the yoke, and to get nimbly back again into the chariot."

All of which sounds simple and delightful. In practice, however, it did not often "work out." For too frequently the wheels of the chariots became clogged, sometimes they jammed in the wheels of other chariots—not necessarily the enemy's—and frequently the horses, driven to frenzy by pain and terror, stampeded on all sides.

Therefore the "steadiness of infantry," of which Cæsar talks so glibly, must in many instances have existed purely in his imagination, and there can be little doubt that the warriors, carried away *nolens volens* by their frenzied horses, often "retreated readily to their own side" long before the enemy pressed them to do so, a regrettable incident which Cæsar passes over with perfunctory comment. And perhaps he is not to be found fault with for doing this, seeing that similar tactics have been indulged in by many of the most successful of our military strategists of modern times.

Probably by Cæsar's time the practice of placing a covering of some sort upon the backs of "saddle" horses had become quite common, at least amongst the Romans.

Among German tribes the use of any sort of covering was still not merely laughed to scorn, but deemed to be actually effeminate, disgraceful and a mark of laziness.

To do the Germans justice, they thoroughly acted up to their theory in this connection, for never, when riding bareback, did they fear to attack cavalry equipped with the horsecloth termed an *ephippion*, which means literally a horse cover.

Referring again to war chariots, Diodorus tells us almost in so many words that the Celts of Gaul and of Northern Italy went to war in two-horse chariots down to quite a late date, after the manner of the Homeric Acheans. These chariots held each two warriors, or a warrior and a charioteer. One of the occupants first hurled a spear at the enemy and then quickly alighted to finish the attack on foot; the other occupant managed the car.

Though Horace himself was not a practical horseman, the views which he expressed upon the subject of horses and of horsemanship are for the most part admirable. In common with Xenophon he deemed good hoofs to be an essential. Listen to the following rather amusing though at the same time quite sensible observations uttered by Horace in one of his famous "Satires": —

"Swells," he writes, "when they buy horses, have a way of covering them up when they look over them, for fear that a handsome shape set upon tender feet, as often happens, may take in the buyer as he hangs open-mouthed over fine haunches, small head, and stately neck. And they are right."

At this time the ancients did not shoe their horses, though it is generally believed that the Romans often covered the hoofs of their mules with a sort of cap made of leather, which they then tied about the fetlock.

These caps or coverings were named *soleæ*, and in the majority of cases had a thin plate or sole made of iron. Nero is said to have used for his 2000 mules plates made of silver instead of iron, and Pliny declares in his famous "Natural History" that Nero's ridiculous wife, Poppæa, used plates of gold for the same purpose.

It seems more than likely that caps of this pattern may have been worn by some at least of the horses of the immortal Ten Thousand, for it is recorded that during the great retreat an Armenian explained to a group of Greeks how best to protect their horses' feet when snow lay thick upon the ground, and the way he recommended was to wrap them up as described.

In the early history of Ireland we find references. There is an Irish epic cycle said to be quite one of the oldest known — the cycle of Cuchulainn — in which the warriors all fight from chariots and do terrible things. In this respect the poems of the Ossianic cycle are different, from which it has been inferred that the latter were written later.

If this was so it helps to bear out the argument that chariots went steadily out of use as cavalry came more and more into vogue. Various dates have been assigned to the "Cuchulainn Saga," but from the records that exist it seems safe to say that the original poem must have been written in Pagan times — the events referred to in it are supposed to have occurred about the first century B.C. — though probably it was revised and added to in later years.

Indeed it is beyond dispute that as early as the seventh century A.D. some of these poems were already deemed to be of great antiquity.

Cuchulainn's horses are described at length in "The Wooing of Emer." They were "alike in size, beauty, fierceness and speed. Their manes were long and curly, and they had curling tails. The right-hand horse was a grey horse, broad in the haunches, fierce, swift and wild; the other was jet-black, his head firmly knit, and he was broad-hoofed and slender; long and curly were his mane and tail. Down his broad forehead hung heavy curls of hair."

We are further told "that was the one chariot which the host of the horses of the chariots of Ulster could not follow on account of the swiftness and speed of the chariot and of the chariot chief who sat in it."

These peerless animals were guided by "two firm-plaited yellow reins," and presumably the black with "long and curly mane and tail" was of Spanish or Gaulish blood.

Soon after the coming of Christ, or probably about the year 60 A.D., a tribe referred to as the Iceni is known to have lived on what is now called Newmarket Heath, and to have owned horses, apparently in great numbers.

Tacitus speaks of the Iceni, who must have been a greater and more powerful people than the majority of modern historians lead us to infer. Again, it is interesting to note that nearly all the gold and silver coins of the Iceni bear upon one side the impression of a horse. Cæsar refers to the Iceni as a race that dwelt in Cambridgeshire, Huntingdonshire, Norfolk and Suffolk, and Tacitus wrote practically to the same effect.

Though horse racing is spoken of incidentally as having been indulged in early in the Anglo-Saxon era, quite the earliest *bonâ-fide* horse races that took place in England, of which we have authentic record, were those organised about the time of the Emperor Severus Alexander, or towards the beginning of the third century A.D. The meeting was held at Netherby, in Yorkshire.

These races were run apparently not long before the assassination of the ill-starred emperor in 222 by the soldiers whom Maximus had corrupted. At other stations as well horse races took place during the Roman occupation, and Carleon, Silchester, Rushborough and Dorchester are mentioned as being among the localities which had to do with the very primitive "Turf" of that period.

Perhaps the undeniable superiority of the British thoroughbred over the horses of other nations to-day may in a measure be due to the time and attention the Romans of that era devoted to the importation of horses of Eastern blood. This seems more likely still to be the case when we remember that the majority of the best of the English mares were crossed with Arabian stallions in the years that followed, and that a succession of such stallions was imported throughout the early and the Middle Ages, and from that time onward right down through the sixteenth, seventeenth and eighteenth centuries, as we shall see presently.

By the beginning of the era of the Saxon kings an Arab steed had come to be looked upon as a recognised royal gift. According to one authority, indeed, Boadicea, the intrepid queen who led the Iceni against the Roman invaders, was greatly attached to her horses.

Most likely she was attached to them, however, only because they helped her so materially in her raids upon her enemies. To pretend that "the sturdy queen," as one historian nicknames her, harboured anything in the least approaching a sympathetic or a sentimental affection for any particular horse would be the acme of all that is grotesque.

Haydn has the misplaced gallantry to allude to Boadicea as "the heroic queen." That her good fortune in possessing horses with considerable staying power enabled her to win her great victory at Verulam is now common history. Therefore we read with the more interest that "this relentless queen destroyed London and other places, slaughtering many Romans, but at last she was overcome near London, by Suetonius, and she ended by committing suicide."

In the second century A.D. the Arabs probably had not begun to breed horses, for at that time we do not hear of Arab horses being held in the high esteem with which they later came to be regarded by the British nation.

Yet even before this, or towards the middle of the first century A.D., the sport of chariot racing had become immensely popular, and the sums spent upon organising the races, training the horses that were to be entered for competition, and in purchasing prizes to be bestowed upon the victors, may justly be said to have been enormous if we bear in mind the purchasing value of the coinage of the period.

That the Romans were given to sacrificing horses to their gods, Pliny the elder has made plain to us. He is said to have written an exhaustive work upon steeds of a certain stamp, but unfortunately the book must have been destroyed in the eruption of Vesuvius in 79 A.D., when Pompeii and Herculaneum were buried, and some 200,000 human beings killed, among them Pliny.

As he points out in his "Natural History," however, the sacrifices of horses took place frequently, especially upon occasions of public solemnity, and he mentions that horses to be immolated were not allowed to be touched even by the Flamen.

Whether or no the Romans habitually sacrificed white horses, after the manner of the Greeks, Illyrians and

Persians, is not stated. They did, however, harness white horses to their chariots upon these and other state occasions, and thus we read that when Julius Cæsar returned from Africa the quadriga in which he drove was, by order of the Senate, drawn by milk-white steeds.

Tacitus tells us that on some occasions when a distinguished chief died the dead man's horse was cremated on the funeral pyre beside its master's body, and we know that the superstitious beliefs of the Persians were upon a par with those of their Germanic kinsmen in so far as the immolation of horses was concerned.

In some instances alleged divination of the future was brought about by the aid of horses. Tacitus himself remarks that it was peculiar to this people (the Germans) "to seek from horses omens and monitions."

"Kept at the public expense in these same woods and groves," he continues, "are white horses, pure from the taint of earthly labour. These are yoked to a sacred chariot and accompanied by the priests and the king, or chief of the tribe, who note their neighings and snortings. No species of divination is more to be trusted, not only by the people and by the nobility, but also by the priests, who regard themselves as the ministers of the gods, and the horses as acquainted with their will."

Amusing, but probably more or less fictitious, stories of Incitatus, the notorious horse of the Roman emperor, Caligula, have been handed down to us. That this beast had the absurd honour conferred upon it of being elected priest and consul we must believe, and there probably is truth in the statement that it ate regularly out of an ivory manger and drank from a golden pail.

CALIGULA ON HORSEBACK. ABOUT 37 A.D.
From a figure in the British Museum

But we must accept with reservation the story that the
horse alone had eighteen attendants in gorgeous apparel or

livery to attend to it. Almost equally fantastic are the tales told of the famous horse that belonged to the Roman emperor, Verus, in the second century A.D. Celer by name, it ate nothing but almonds and raisins, and its stable was a suite of apartments in the emperor's principal palace. In place of horse clothing it wore a garment of royal purple.

I need hardly repeat that these and similar stories that have been handed down to us must be received with considerable scepticism.

A description, probably true, of what were deemed in the first century A.D. to be the best points about a horse, is to be found in the "Eclogues." The lines, translated, run somewhat as follows: —

> "My beast displays
> A deep-set back; a head and neck
> That tossing proudly feel no check
> From over-bulk; feet fashioned slight,
> Thin flanks, and brow of massive height;
> While in its narrow horny sheath
> A well-turned hoof is bound beneath."

Towards the middle of the fourth century A.D. the popularity of what must be described as circus riding would seem to have increased rather suddenly, and we read that at about this time the Sicilian horses were nearly as much in demand for public performances and processions as the Cappadocian and the Spanish. Though such performances must have been primitive indeed by comparison with even the simpler of the feats we see performed to-day, they were then deemed marvellous in the extreme, and people came from far and near to witness them.

This probably was in a measure due to the general love of riding that prevailed amongst the wealthier classes at that period. Indeed the possession of a large stud of horses was in many parts of Greece, and especially in Athens, considered the hall-mark of what we should term to-day a man of culture, in the same way that the possession of horses, hounds and hawks was supposed to mark the aristocrat in Mediæval times.

Thus a man often would be named after the class of horse he owned. Xanthippus meant "He of the dun horses"; Leucippus, "He of the white horses"; and Melanippus, "He of the black horses."

———————————

By the close of the fourth century A.D. the Romans apparently had outgrown their prejudice against the use of saddles, for at about that time the saddle is referred to with some frequency. Certain it is that in 380 A.D. the famous cavalrymen of Theodosius were mounted on horses provided with true saddles—that is to say saddles with a tree, also with a bow in front and behind.

Generally a cloth or numner was worn beneath saddles, but it is known that at one time Roman horses suffered from sore backs owing probably to the way the Roman soldiers sat their horses when saddles first came into vogue. Soon after this it was that the saddle came to be known as "the chair," presumably because of the Latin word *sella*, from which we have the French noun, *selle*, meaning saddle.

Some famous horses are referred to in the records of the sixth century, but little is said of their history. Thus we have the Persian steed of Chosroes, called Shibdiz, a name signifying "fleeter than the wind." Apparently he was a famous charger, for we read that he carried his master safely through several important engagements. Yet he was used for other purposes.

The story of King Arthur is so closely bound up with fable and fiction that the truth is difficult to get at. He must have owned many good horses, however, of which Spumador—a word signifying "the foaming one"—and the mare Lamri were perhaps the most renowned. There are, nevertheless, historians who maintain that these horses never actually existed.

Sir Tristram's charger, Passe Brewell, mentioned in the "History of King Arthur," and elsewhere, is another animal around which "a web of imaginative description," as one writer terms it has been woven. Consequently we shall be well advised to pass these fables by without comment.

In the first half of the sixth century the practice of regularly shoeing horses apparently came into vogue, for shoes are referred to in the records of the ways and customs of the famous Emperor Justinian. It seems certain, however, that the shoes fashioned at about that period were clumsy in design, also needlessly heavy. Specimens of them have from time to time been discovered, and it is said one was found in the tomb of King Childeric, the date of whose death is placed so far back as 460 A.D.

Though Tacitus, who wrote between 80 and 116 A.D., does not allude to the horses of the Swedes, it is certain that about the sixth century A.D. the Swedes had become not only a race of fine horsemen, but owners of magnificent horses. Indeed in 550 A.D., or thereabouts, Jornandes went so far as to compare them favourably with the race of Thuringians.

Probably it was in a measure owing to the intense devotion of the Swedish king, Adhils, to horses and to all

94

that appertained to them that the Swedish nation became so renowned for their horses and their horsemanship. Then, though the Arabs had no horses at the beginning of the Christian era, they probably were breeding them in great numbers by the beginning of the sixth century A.D., for it was due mainly to a quarrel at about that time over a famous horse named Dahis that two formidable tribes entered into a deadly and long-drawn-out struggle.

At about this period the Romans began to pay almost fastidious attention to the colour of their horses. The colour most preferred for a war horse was dark brown, chestnut, or bay, with a white blaze up the face, or a white patch or star upon the forehead. Light-coloured horses were avoided as much as possible, except when the animals were needed for processions, and so forth.

A graphic description is given of a fierce combat between approximately 1000 of Justinian's cavalry, led by the renowned general, Belisarius, and an equal number of Goths.

The latter, determined to enter Rome, had crossed the Tiber, when the column of Belisarius came upon them suddenly.

The engagement began at once.

We are told that "Belisarius himself fought like a common soldier," as the bravest of the chiefs of that period sometimes did. He was astride one of his favourite and best-trained chargers, a horse described as having "all his body dark-coloured, but his face pure white from the top of the head to the nose."

An animal so marked was termed by the Greeks *phalios*, and by the barbarians *balas*, words signifying "bald." While the battle was in progress a number of Belisarius' soldiers left his ranks and joined the Goths'. Thus it came about that suddenly Belisarius heard shouts from the enemy's lines, and the cries distinctly audible:

"Belisarius rides the bald-faced horse! Strike him! Slay it!"

And most likely the bald-faced horse and his gallant rider would have been slaughtered had Belisarius' bodyguard not hastened to rally round him and eventually succeeded in beating off his assailants, many of whom, earlier in the day, had fought beside him.

CHAPTER V

THE coming of Mahomet, who announced himself prophet about the year 611 A.D., marks an epoch in the history of nations, and it serves also as a landmark, if one may express it so, in the horse's progress in its bearing upon the world's history.

At intervals throughout the Koran, which Mahomet compiled probably about 610, we come upon direct allusions to the horse in the part it played at that time in the growth of what must be termed civilisation. Probably Mahomet realised more fully than any of his contemporaries how indispensable to the human race the horse had by this time become, for in one passage in the Koran he puts a strange utterance into the mouth of the Almighty, whom he represents as apostrophising the horse, telling it that it shall be "for man a source of happiness and wealth," adding, "thy back shall be a seat of honour, and thy belly of riches, and every grain of barley given to thee shall purchase indulgence for the sinner," while in another place he declares that "every grain of barley given to a horse is entered by God in the Register of Good Works."

He describes in an interesting way the horse of the

Archangel Gabriel, to which the name Haizum was given, also Dhuldul, the peerless steed of his son-in-law, Ali, and his own milk-white mule, Fadda. All this is the more remarkable when we bear in mind that in the centuries that preceded Mahomet's birth the Arab race was practically a nonentity in so far as the continual struggles for supremacy in Egypt and in Western Asia were concerned, when the great Assyrian, Babylonian, Egyptian, Persian, Median, Roman and Macedonian tribes fought with such dogged determination and proved each in turn more or less victorious.

Yet it is more than likely—some of our leading historians pronounce positively upon this point—that if in the years just before Mahomet's birth the tribes had not become possessed of a staunch race of horses, and devoted much time to perfecting themselves in horsemanship in the true meaning of the term, Islam would have remained unchanged instead of almost revolutionising the world in the way it did.

Small wonder, therefore, that Mahomet was enthusiastic —unduly enthusiastic many even among his disciples maintained him to be—in striving to promote among his own people a fondness for horses. Undoubtedly it was owing to this that when at last Mahomet died some of the best-bred steeds in existence were to be found among the horses in the region of Nejd.

In Mahomet's era it was that stirrups first came to be used regularly by both cavalry and what were termed "private horsemen"—the latter we should to-day call civilians. True stirrups most likely were invented and introduced by the Teutonic people of the Lower Rhine and the region adjoining, for we know there was no Latin or Greek term for a stirrup, and as the Teutonic tribes were large men of heavy build they naturally would be much more likely to feel the need of assistance when mounting than would men of small stature, light and agile, who must have been able to vault on to their horses without difficulty.

The English term "stirrup" probably is a contraction of the early English "stige-rap," a word that comes from "stigan," to mount, and "rap," rope—in short, a mounting-rope. In the eighth century A.D. the Angles were using saddle horses in large numbers, according to the Venerable Bede, some of whose writings, however, are said not to bear the impress of strict veracity. Yet it is probable that he speaks of what he knew when he tells us that about the year 631 A.D. "the English first began to saddle horses," while many of the horsemen who opposed the incursion of the hordes of Romans are known beyond dispute to have been mounted on saddled horses.

Mention of the mare, Alborak, called also Borak, must be made—though only a mythical animal—as she was said to have carried Mahomet from earth into the seventh heaven. "She was milk-white," we are told, like Fadda, the mule, with "the wings of an eagle and a human face with a horse's cheeks," while "every pace she took was equal to the farthest range of human sight." In Arabic the word means literally "the lightning."

Procopius, who wrote in the sixth century A.D., is looked upon generally as a dependable authority, and probably upon most occasions he wrote the truth. Yet he would seem to have made one or two rather grave misstatements when speaking of the horse in its relation to the history of his time.

In an interesting way he describes certain stirring scenes in the war between the Angli who had settled in Britain and the Varni—the Werini of the "Leges Barbarorum"—whose region lay chiefly east of the Rhine. The direct cause of this war was the positive refusal of the king of the Varni to marry an Anglian princess to whom he had been affianced for a considerable time.

"These islanders," wrote Procopius, referring to the Angli, "are the most valiant of all the barbarians with whom we are acquainted, and they fight on foot. For not only do they not know how to ride, but it is their lot not even to know what a horse is like, since in this island they do not see a horse, even in a picture, for this animal seems never to have existed in Britain. But if at any time it should happen that some of them, either on an embassy, or for some other reason, should be living with Romans or Franks, or with anyone else that hath horses, and it should there be necessary for them to ride on horseback, they are unable to mount, but other men have to help them up and set them on their horses' backs; and again, when they wish to dismount, they have to be lifted, and set down on the ground. Neither are the Varni horsemen, but they too are all infantry. Such then are these barbarians."

Clearly he misstated facts in this instance, for it is beyond dispute that horses were known in Britain at the time to which he refers. For the rest the description may be considered more or less accurate.

It is interesting to note in this connection that whereas in the tombs of the Anglo-Saxons the shield and the weapons of the buried warrior are usually discovered, bits and harness are found in these tombs in rare instances only. On the other hand in the Scandinavian barrows in Scotland the bones of men and horses mixed have been discovered frequently.

100

Perhaps the first historical allusion to horse racing, as we understand it now, and to "running" horses, as race horses continued to be called for many centuries afterwards, is the one that occurs in the ninth century A.D., when Hugh, the founder of the royal house of Capet, in France, made a present of running horses to King Athelstan in the hope that in return the king might allow him to wed his sister, Ethelswitha.

Hengist and Horsa are said by some historians to have displayed interest in horse racing, but the statement is not based upon indisputable evidence, any more than the assertion that because Hengist and Horsa are alleged by one historian at least to have given the order that forms of horses should be cut upon the chalk hills of Berkshire therefore all the Saxon banners must have borne as a device a white horse.

The white horse at Wantage other historians declare to have been cut in commemoration of Alfred's great victory over the Danes at the battle of Æscendun or Ashtreehill, during the reign of his brother, Ethelred I. Its length is 374 feet, and even at a distance of nearly fifteen miles it is distinctly visible in clear weather. This recalls to mind the device of the House of Hanover—a white horse galloping; and of the House of Savoy—a white horse rampant.

Mention must here be made of the immortal Roland and his equally famous horse, Veillantiff, though owing to the pair have figured so largely in romance the actual truth about them can be traced only with difficulty.

We may take it for granted, however, that Roland was the son of Milo, Duke of Aiglant; that he was Count of Mans and Knight of Blaives; and that his mother was Bertha, the sister of Charlemagne. Orlando is the name by which he is known in Italian romance; Vegliantino the name of his horse; and he figures prominently in Theroulde's "Chanson de Roland," in the romance, "Chroniq de Turpin," and of course in Ariosto's epic of Mad Roland and Boiardo's "Orlando in Love." He was said to be eight feet tall and to have "an open countenance which invited confidence and inspired respect," also to have been "brave, loyal and simple-minded."

The story of his slaying at Fronsac, in single combat, the Saracen tyrant and giant, Angoulaffre, as described in "Croquemitaine," naturally is fiction. He desired, it was said, by way of reward to marry Aude, the fair daughter of Sir Gerard and Lady Guibourg, but Roland was slain at Roncesvalles in the Pyrenees during the return march from Saragossa, while in command of the rear-guard, being caught "together with the flower of the French chivalry" in an ambuscade and massacred to a man. Aude is said to have died of grief upon hearing the news.

Roland's horse, Veillantiff, must have been an incomparable charger and more intelligent than even his master, for it is related that whenever Roland was hard pressed Veillantiff obtained knowledge of the fact in some mysterious way and at once carried Roland out of danger so far as he was able.

Equally intelligent in this respect was the charger named Orelia, owned by Roderick, the last of the Goths. According to Southey this horse too was renowned for its shape and speed. Indeed Southey based the story of his famous epic upon the historical record of the defeat of Roderick in 711 A.D., at the battle of Guadalete, near Xeres de la Frontera. Roderick, the thirty-fourth and last of the old Visigothic kings, himself attributed his victories in a great measure to the courage of his horses, and apparently he was proud of all his horses for we read that he "bitterly bemoaned the death of any one of them." Another remarkable and famous steed was Trebizond, the grey charger of Admiral Guarinos, one of the French knights taken prisoner at Roncesvalles.

Alfana, the clever mare mentioned in Ariosto's "Orlando Furioso" as belonging to Gradasso, King of Sericana, whom Ariosto describes as "the bravest of the Pagan knights," has many legends attached to it.

Thus upon occasions Gradasso who, though famous as a knight, was an unconscionable bully, would treat Alfana with grotesque kindness, at other times beating it unmercifully; and when, with 100,000 vassals in his train, "all discrowned kings"(!) who never addressed him except upon their knees, he went to war against Charlemagne, the mare, Alfana, played a prominent part.

<hr/>

Though in these pages but few allusions have been made to the horses of mythology, modern interest in mythological history being at a very low ebb, the mysterious eight-legged grey steed of Odin, chief god of Scandinavia, must not be passed unnoticed. His name was Sleipnir, and inasmuch as he could travel over earth and ocean he was deemed to be typical of the wind that blows over land and water from eight principal and far-distant points.

According to Beowulf—composed probably in the eighth century—the Scandinavians set great value upon their steeds, especially upon their dun-coloured horses, their apple-dun horses and their white horses. Therefore it seems almost odd that the early Norse settlers in Iceland should have indulged as largely as they undoubtedly did in the brutal "sport" of horse fighting, a form of amusement that to this day is in vogue in parts of Siam.

The saga of Burnt Njal, with its scene laid in the tenth century, refers repeatedly to incidents in which the horse plays a chief part. The description of the mighty encounter between the horse of Starkad and the horse of Gunnar of Lithend is peculiarly disagreeable, but as it gives us probably a very accurate idea of the way in which these horse battles were arranged and carried out, it is worth quoting almost in full.

Starkad, we are told, had "a good horse of chestnut hue, and it was thought that no horse was his match in fight." The horse that Gunnar of Lithend decided to pit against it was a brown. It is practically upon the result of this fight that the famous tragedy turns.

"And now men ride to the horse fight," we read, "and a very great crowd was gathered together. Gunnar and his friends were there, and Starkad and his sons.... Gunnar was in a red kirtle, and had about his loins a broad belt, and a riding rod in his hand. Then the horses ran at one another, and bit each other long, so that there was no need for anyone to touch them, and that was the greatest sport! Then Thorgeir and Kol made up their minds that they would push their horse forward just as the horses rushed together, and see if Gunnar would fall before him.

"Now the horses ran at one another again, and both Thorgeir and Kol ran alongside their horse's flank. Gunnar pushed his horse against them, and what happened in a trice was this, that Thorgeir and his brother fell flat down on their backs, and their horse atop of them!"

Soon after this the horse battle developed into a serious encounter between the partisans of the respective animals, with the result that Gunnar's horse had an eye gouged out by Thorgeir. In the library at Reykjavik a very interesting picture representing a horse battle of this kind is still to be seen.

———————

We have now seen how, from the very earliest time until the eve of the Norman Conquest, the horse played a prominent part in the world's history. More than any other animal it had helped, either directly or indirectly, to bring about great victories, to develop and strengthen the courage of nations, to mould the character of men, and to add in several ways to life's pleasure.

That the horse should have been almost worshipped by the very tribes who offered up living horses as sacrifices to their gods has been pronounced paradoxical by some writers; yet there was nothing inconsistent about this, for in all times when sacrifices have been common those offering sacrifice have given what they most cherished or esteemed.

What is remarkable is the fact that, of all animals known to have existed in the different countries and in the different regions of those countries to which reference has been made, the horse stands alone as man's direct assistant, one might say ally; and, in addition, the horse is the one animal with a history traceable through the early centuries, owing to the almost unbroken line of references made to it in the story of the human race and progress towards civilisation.

How far advanced the world would have been at the time of the Conqueror's landing, how far advanced it would be to-day, had the horse not played so prominent a part in its development, none can say. There can be no doubt, however, but that the human race would have advanced far more slowly had the employment of horses been withheld.

Of mythical horses that have "existed," the name is

legion. To deal at length with these strange creatures would need a volume half as large as this is. I have mentioned that few save scholars to-day take interest in mythology, so I shall refer only to some half-a-dozen of the many horses of fable and of mythology whose names are household words.

Pegasus, the winged horse of Apollo and the Muses, is perhaps the best known by repute. The name of course is Greek, and means, more or less, "one born near the ocean," and according to the famous fable Perseus rode Pegasus when rescuing Andromeda.

Frequently in history we find a ship alluded to as "Perseus' flying horse." Thus in the story of the destruction of Troy, "Perseus conquered the head of Medusa, and did make Pegase, the most swift ship, which he always calls Perseus' flying horse," while Shakespeare in *Troilus and Cressida* speaks of "The strong-ribbed bark through liquid mountains cut ... like Perseus' horse."

How Perseus beheaded Medusa, chief of the Gorgons, and how everyone who afterwards looked at the head with its hair turned into snakes by the jealous goddess Minerva was then and there transformed into stone is too well known to need repetition at length here.

Selene, the moon goddess, usually represented in a chariot drawn by fiery white horses—to some extent this is inconsistent, seeing that from time almost immemorial white horses have notoriously been the least fiery of any—must be mentioned, for the famous cast or model of Selene's horse shown in the British Museum indicates clearly the stamp of animal that was most highly prized about that period. According to Greek mythology, Selene was in love with the setting sun, Endymion, and bore him fifty daughters in addition to those she bore the god Zeus.

Achilles' remarkable steed, Xanthos, was, we are told, "human to all intents." When "severely spoken to" by its master because on the battlefield it had deserted Patroclos, the horse first "looked about him sadly," and then, according to the "Iliad," it told Achilles with a reproachful expression in its eyes that he too would soon be dead, for that this was "the inexorable decree of destiny"—a prophecy that came true.

Achilles owned also the wonderful horse, Balios, which first of all Neptune had given to Peleus. The sire of Balios, like the sire of Xanthos, was the West Wind, its dam the harpy, Swift Foot.

According to Virgil the famous horse of Greek mythology, Cyllaros, belonged to Pollux, and was named after Cylla, in Troas. Ovid, however affirms that it belonged to Castor, for in his "Metamorphose" he says, when speaking of Cyllaros, that "He, O Castor, was a courser worthy thee ... coal-black his colour, but like jet it shone: His legs and flowing tail were white alone." Then, Adrastos was saved at the siege of Thebes by a horse famous for its speed and given to him by Hercules. Its name was Arion, and Neptune was said to have caused it to rise out of the earth, using his trident as a magic wand. The name is Greek for "martial," hence the signification, "war horse," given to it in this instance. We read that "its right feet were those of a human creature," "it spoke with a human voice," and "ran with incredible swiftness."

Perhaps one of the most notorious horses of Persian mythology is Reksh, a steed that belonged to Rustam, the Persian Hercules, son of Zal, and Prince of Sedjistan. Rustam became famous chiefly on account of his great battle with the white dragon, Asdeev. The description of Rustam's deadly encounter with his son, Sohrab—it ended in the latter's death—is described in Matthew Arnold's poem, "Sohrab and Rustam" in very fine language.

―――――――――――

But even these few references to horses of mythology may be pronounced dull reading in this prosaic age, so for the present I will leave the subject and come down to earth once more. It is interesting to learn that the Arab race, apparently from the time when it first began to breed horses, was wont to trace the pedigrees of its horses through the dams and not through the sires, in the same way that in ancient days this people traced its own lineage. The reason the Arabs did so remains to this day a moot point, though it would seem almost certain that in common with the Veneti they believed the selection of the dam to be of more vital importance than the selection of the stallion in order to secure good stock.

Indeed even now there are races who hold this view, and to confirm their opinion they quote Aristotle, who also maintained that pedigrees ought by rights to be traced through the female line. Nor are they at all peculiar, for some of the foremost among modern breeders of horses hold that in almost every case the qualities of the dam descend more directly than do those of the sire.

We have now come to what may be termed the second period of the horse in history—the period that begins with William the Conqueror's reign and ends with the Stuart Period. From very early centuries down to the coming of Christ, and from the coming of Christ down to the Norman invasion, all the records bearing directly upon the horse in its relation to the world's progress are necessarily open to criticism, for almost all historical records of that period have to be accepted with some reserve.

It may be said, indeed, that no two historians prior to the Conquest can be found who agree in detail one with the other, while some there are whose statements are almost diametrically opposed. In compiling these pages, therefore, I have tried to use discretion.

―――――――――

Apparently an impression is prevalent amongst historians that the horses of the centuries before the Conquest, and therefore presumably also the horses of the period that preceded the birth of Christ, lived longer than those of later times.

What can have given rise to this idea it is hard to say, and that the belief most likely is fallacious we are led to infer from the statements of those early writers who state definitely the ages at which their favourite chargers died.

Yet at least two of our modern historians assert that the horses of the early Greeks and Romans lived to the age of thirty-five or more, upon an average.

That such misstatement should continue to be handed down is very regrettable; while equally to be deprecated is the habit common more especially among the younger school of French historians of applying the principles of the higher criticism in cases where such criticism *ipso facto* cannot hold good, the result being that conclusions are arrived at which in many instances are wholly false.

To take a single case in point—rather a well-known Continental antiquary mentions in his historical essays that during the period approximately between the coming of Christ and the reign of William the Conqueror horses practically the world over "went out of use more and more."

By "the world over" he means, of course, as much of the world as was known in those days, but the statement is none the less incorrect, and it seems clear that he must have come to this false conclusion through inferring that because in certain regions the designs upon the ancient monuments, and in some instances the figures upon the coinage, represent a horse, or horses and chariots, the monuments and coins of a later date show only an unmounted warrior.

The true reason of this, however, probably is that the later monuments were erected, and the later coins struck, at a period when neither famous battles were being fought nor great contests of skill decided. Students of history well know, indeed, that the monarchs as well as the great chiefs and leaders in the early centuries before the Conquest, and to some extent in the centuries after it, almost invariably commemorated upon their monuments, coins and parchments such events as happened to be of importance at the moment, or, as we should say to-day, of passing interest only.

Indeed, as I have endeavoured to show, one of the most noticeable features about the horse in its relation to history is the manner in which it gradually influenced the development of the various nations. The early Libyan horses were famous for what must be described as their gentleness and their intelligence, characteristics which apparently marked some of the Libyan races.

The horses of Europe, on the other hand, were vicious in various ways, and less tractable, but also they were less timid than the Libyan horses.

It is curious to read, then, that the European races that owned these horses had several characteristics in common. In addition it is well known that in the *mêlée* of a battle the horses of the contending armies quite commonly bit savagely one at another, and some of the early writers whose utterances can be relied upon maintain that even in the thick of the fight such horses but rarely bit or savaged horses other than the enemy's, and the enemy themselves.

Another point worth noting is that though often in the early ages horses were immolated, yet deliberate cruelty to a horse upon other occasions was almost universally condemned by law. No precautions, however, were taken for the prevention of cruelty to any other sort of animal.

This is, in itself, significant, for it can hardly be supposed that unnecessary cruelty to horses was condemned from the standpoint of the humanitarian. Probably it was the horse's usefulness to mankind that served to guard him against ill-usage, and, as we shall see presently, it was this same usefulness that protected him from ill-treatment in centuries long after the Conquest.

Indeed there are parts of the world where to this day horses are well treated because to ill-use them is deemed unwise policy. Thus in no part of the Western States of America have I ever seen a horse flogged unmercifully, and upon several occasions when attention has been drawn to this the reply has been practically the same: "If we served them badly we should get less work out of them," an observation that some Englishmen, plenty of Frenchmen, and very many Italians, who have to do with horses, might with advantage bear in mind.

———————

The physical strength of horses in the very early centuries must have been prodigious. If the details we have of the way in which the early war chariots were constructed are accurate, then at least three of our twentieth-century horses

111

would be needed to accomplish the work, one might almost say perform the feats, that a pair of horses could do twelve or thirteen centuries ago.

Even as late in the world's history as the period of Julius Cæsar the staying power of some of the war horses in Britain was amazing. Men who have been in action in our own times will tell you that a wounded horse gives in at once, that he seems to have no heart. Yet in Julius Cæsar's time, and in earlier epochs, an arrow or a javelin wound, if not too severe, apparently had the effect of setting a war horse upon his mettle rather than of causing him to give in.

Can the horse's temperament, then, have changed within the last ten centuries? Is he a less courageous animal than he was? Is he more highly strung, less intelligent, less strong physically, and of a weaker constitution? Such problems have to do with the history of the horse rather than with the horse in history, and, so far as I am aware, they have not as yet been solved.

PART II

FROM THE CONQUEST TO THE STUART PERIOD

CHAPTER I

THE beginning of William the Conqueror's reign marks a turning-point in the story of the horse's influence upon the British nation, also, incidentally, in the general development of the horse.

Roger de Bellesne, Earl of Shrewsbury, who is said to have been an accomplished horseman — as fine horsemanship was understood in those days — obtained leave of the king to import from Spain a number of stallions of great value.

These stallions, indeed, were said at the time to be "the best procurable in Spain," and we are told that when King William beheld them he displayed great delight, at the same time "expressing his approval in a very forcible way."

The king himself apparently was not a finished horseman; yet he had a strong liking for horses, possibly in the same way that "he loved the great deer of the forests as though he had been their father"(!) Most likely he was too heavily built a man to make a graceful rider, though it is said that upon the arrival of Lord Shrewsbury's stallions he went on horseback to inspect them, and, as we know, towards the end of the sixteenth or the beginning of the seventeenth century the poet Drayton praised very highly the progeny of these same horses.

Naturally this importation of valuable stallions greatly improved the breed of horses in Britain, and from the time of the Conquest onward the improvement was distinctly noticeable.

———

Though some historians tell us that the Anglo-Saxons rode on horseback, others maintain that they did not ride. There can be no doubt, however, that they did not fight on horseback. The well-known scene on Bayeux tapestry that represents the battle of Hastings shows us Harold fighting on foot when the arrow strikes him in the eye.

A comparatively modern historian has tried to disprove the popular story of the Normans shooting their shafts high into the air so that in their descent these shafts might pierce the heads of the enemy, but the old narrative is still believed by the great body of modern students.

King William's warriors were, of course, almost all mounted—of that there cannot be a doubt. Had they not been the Saxons would most likely have won the day, even though the enemy was clad in mail. Also it should be remembered that the cavalry brought over by King William was practically of the stamp that some three centuries earlier had resisted very firmly the Moslem attack at Poictiers. The chargers were of the same stock, and therefore it may with truth be said that the famous Norman Conquest and the great and important events that followed it in the history of this country were directly due to the simple fact that the Normans possessed war horses and knew thoroughly how to manage them.

Of precisely what stamp the Normans' chargers were that

were imported at this time cannot be said for certain. Without doubt, however, they were tall and heavily built animals, for the armed men they had to carry were all of very great weight.

For ten, or possibly twelve centuries a breed of great horses had been multiplying largely in the northern and western regions of Europe, so the inference is that the cavalry of the Normans must have been of that breed.

Also the saddles they are represented as wearing were extremely massive and presumably of great weight. Those shown on the Bayeux tapestry have a deep curve which must have made them difficult to fall out of, and we are told by Giraldus that saddles almost exactly similar, and provided with stirrups, were in use in Ireland a century or so later. The riders at that time wore high boots, prick spurs, and hauberk.

BAYEUX TAPESTRY SUPPOSED TO REPRESENT THE BATTLE OF HASTINGS. 1066

A monk of Canterbury, William Stephanides, writing early in the reign of Henry II., alludes to various kinds of horses used in Great Britain, and among these there undoubtedly were some of the stamp that the Normans imported.

"Without one of the London city gates," he tells us, "is a certain smooth field"—no doubt the site known to-day as Smithfield—"and every Friday there is a brave sight of gallant horses to be sold. Many come from the city to buy or look on—to wit, earls, barons, knights and citizens. There are to be found here managed or war horses (*dextrarii*), of elegant shape, full of fire and giving every proof of a generous and noble temper; likewise cart horses, horses fitted for the dray, or the plough, or the chariot."

From other sources we are able to gather that at this time there must have been many war horses in England, and that they were for the most part animals of great size and strength. Consequently the cavalry of the period were extremely unwieldy. On the other hand we know that the rest of the horses distributed throughout the country were but little bigger than cobs, and we read that though attempts were made to mount men-at-arms on some of them all such attempts had soon to be abandoned, the horses being "oppressed by the weight of the armour and the heavy accoutrements."

Probably this was the reason such strenuous efforts were presently made by the various reigning monarchs, and by the parliaments that were in power between the reign of Henry II. and the reign of Elizabeth, to breed bigger and heavier horses, "great horses" as they came to be called, and are often termed still.

Some of the Latin records of the Mediæval age contain interesting allusions to these great horses, *dextrarii* and *magni equi* they were called. The horses of this stamp do not appear to have been very intelligent animals, but their physical strength was colossal, and in selecting them particular attention was paid to their power of endurance, or, as we call it to-day, their staying power.

Apparently Henry II. and Richard I. were partial to chestnut and dark brown stallions, but King John, and later Queen Elizabeth, preferred black. Indeed we are told that in the beginning of his reign King John vowed he would have his courtiers ride none but black horses, and that the sums he had to pay to enable him to gratify so foolish a fad—it may have been mere vanity—were quoted among the acts of extravagance that later incensed his barons and led ultimately to their making him sign Magna Charta.

As the size and strength of the war horses grew greater in all countries, so did the weight and strength of the armour steadily increase. Towards the end of the twelfth century the Norman hauberk that for many years had proved effective, and that even the most far-seeing of the warriors firmly believed could not be improved upon, began to make way for the heavy chain mail—the most picturesque armour ever adopted by any nation—which, when first introduced, was said to render the warrior almost invulnerable.

But as time went on, and the strength of both men and horses further increased, and the weapons of war became more deadly still, the armour again underwent a change, so that about the beginning of the fourteenth century we find the "perfect armour," as it had come to be called, being in its turn discarded in favour of the hideous plate armour that less than a hundred years afterwards was adopted by practically every "civilised" nation in Europe.

A monk of Canterbury, by name FitzStephen, who in the reign of Henry II. was secretary to the famous Archbishop à

118

Becket, refers incidentally to some rather primitive horse races which took place at Smithfield towards the end of the twelfth century, and in doing so he quaintly tells us that "the jockeys, inspired with thoughts of applause, and in the hope of victory, clap spurs to the willing horses, brandish their whips, and cheer them with their cries!"

Reference is made to these races in several other of the early documents, and though they are among the first horse races of which descriptions have been handed down to us, it seems clear that they attracted a great concourse of spectators and gave rise to much reckless wagering. That the animals entered were all practically untrained is made apparent.

King Richard I. is said to have been a good judge of a horse and to have owned a number of swift-running steeds. Upon one or two occasions he endeavoured to establish horse racing as a national pastime, but the country was not yet ripe for it, and his attempts met with but scant encouragement.

It is said that his courtiers strove to serve their royal master by having recourse to threats in those districts where the introduction of horse racing was opposed, but all to no purpose.

King John, upon ascending the throne, devoted much time to hunting and similar sports, and valued good horses so greatly that in some instances he insisted that the fines he was so fond of extorting should be paid in horses instead of in money.

Then, following in the footsteps of William the Conqueror, he imported a number of stallions, among them many of the Eastern breed, and on the pastures in Kent where the town of Eltham and the village of Mottingham now stand he established the famous stud from which so many of the horses owned in after years by Queen Elizabeth were directly descended.

Worthy of mention here is the coincidence that the early days of some of the most celebrated thoroughbreds of recent times were spent in the very paddocks where King John's foals and imported horses were disporting themselves some seven centuries earlier.

On the subject of the great horses of the Middle Ages it is interesting to read that while British rulers were striving to breed animals which would be both bigger and stronger than their predecessors, the Persians in their country were endeavouring to breed and rear horses on lines precisely similar, and with the same objects in view.

How successful the attempts of the latter proved may be gathered from the fact that, in the centuries that followed, the Persian horses became renowned the world over for their immense strength, though the animals of this particular breed never became famous for their speed.

Indeed the chief victories won by the Persians in their terrific encounters with the Turks in the fifteenth and sixteenth centuries were due in a great measure to the superior size and strength of the Persian war horses, though, of course, the fact that the Turks had only their shields with which to protect themselves must have helped the Persians materially.

Perhaps some of the most interesting and accurate representations of the horses of about this period are those to be found in parts of Ireland among the remains of Irish art. These remains, rather let us call them relics, are almost matchless, and they represent horses driven in chariots, and some mounted by riders.

Thus three horsemen in addition to two chariots with horses harnessed are to be seen on the two panels of the plinth of the historic North Cross at Clonmacnoise in King's County. The wheels of these chariots have eight spokes, and the relic is believed by the foremost of our antiquaries to date back to the tenth century.

A panel almost similar, dating back approximately to the same period, is to be seen on an upright cross in a street in the town of Kells, in County Meath, and on this cross not only are horsemen shown, but in addition a hunting scene is clearly depicted.

Relics such as these help to demonstrate that the interest taken in horses by the people of Great Britain, just before and just after the Conquest, was shared by the natives of Ireland, though not until several centuries had elapsed did the Irish show signs of becoming the thoroughly horse-loving nation that they are to-day.

It is true that from a very early period they were fond of most kinds of outdoor pursuits that need daring in addition to the exercise of skill upon the part of those anxious to become proficient at them. Also it is true that the horse has from first to last had much to do with the moulding of the Irish character.

The horse's immediate bearing upon the history and progress of Ireland begins, however, at a later date, and in the same manner the importation of great horses, and the establishment of what must have been the precursors of our modern stud farms, occur later in Ireland's history than in England's.

———————

With the accession of Henry III. we find upon the throne

a king keenly interested in all that had to do with horses, and devoted to the chase as well as to "stirring contests between competing horses." For authentic particulars of the contests in which these "competing horses" took part we may search the ancient records almost in vain. Apparently the few race meetings organised were, to say the best we can of them, not of great importance, not excepting those in which the king and his nobles were directly interested. To afford opportunities for wagering was, so far as one can gather, their principal *raison d'être*, and such rules of racing as did exist most likely were almost wholly disregarded.

In this respect the king would seem not to have been much more particular than his subjects, though, as already said, information obtainable upon the subject is of the scantiest, and is at best unreliable.

In the history of Henry III.'s reign there occurs what we may take to be the first direct reference to "a village named Newmarket," in Cambridgeshire. As I have already pointed out, the tribe that dwelt on Newmarket Heath in very early times and was known as the Iceni apparently was interested in horses and to some extent bred horses, so it is not astonishing to learn that in the thirteenth century the people then living in Newmarket and the neighbourhood still carried on the traditions of the Iceni, even to boasting openly that steeds bred upon the Heath could not be rivalled for speed "the world over."

This, most likely, was an empty boast, for what could a small community, that presumably travelled but rarely, know at first hand of horses bred even in far distant parts of England?

It is true that Simon de Montfort had a high opinion of the horses bred at Newmarket, for he tells us so in a letter written a few years before his death—he was killed at Evesham in 1265. Presumably he rode in the hunting field some of his horses that had been reared at Newmarket, for he was as keen about hunting as about soldiering.

Historians have described him as "the great patriotic baron of his period," a description that is accurate if we are to judge from his acts. I believe I am right in saying that Simon de Montfort was the first master of foxhounds of whom mention is made in British history, but upon this point I am open to correction. Certainly he is the first of whose life we have authentic details. On his great seal attached to a deed dated 1259, and now in Paris among the royal archives, he is shown galloping beside his hounds, urging them on, and blowing his horn. He is said to have hunted largely in Leicestershire and Warwickshire, and as he lived in the thirteenth century the seal referred to forms most likely the first picture we have of a *bonâ fide* run with foxhounds.

In Blount's "Ancient Tenures," a volume that is extremely interesting and in some respects amusing, we are told that "In the reign of King Edward I. Walter Marescullus paid at the crucem lapideam six horseshoes with nails for a certain building which he held of the king *in capite* opposite the stone cross."

This recalls to mind that in the reign of Henry III., and even later, horseshoes and horseshoe nails were frequently taken in lieu of rent. Whether or no horseshoes were of exceptional value does not appear, but we are led to suppose that they must have been from the fact that in 1251 a farrier named Walter le Brun, who lived in the Strand, in London, was granted a plot of land in the parish of St Clements "to place there a forge, six horseshoes to be paid to the parish every year for the privilege."

In after years the same plot was granted to the Mayor and citizens of London, who, it is said, still render six horseshoes to the Exchequer annually.

According to the Statutes, 25, Edward I., c. 21; and 36, Edward III. cc. 4, 5, the king could commandeer from his subjects as many horses as he might need for his own service. By the nobles and barons this was deemed a harsh measure, and frequently they rebelled against it. Some of the more spirited even refused to acknowledge its validity, with the result that a number were slain whilst attempting to retain their horses by force; others were imprisoned; and a few were put to death as rebels. Indeed at this period the theft of a horse ranked second only to murder, and was punished as severely.

———————

A horse upon whose history several more or less romantic stories and poems have been based was the bay charger owned by King Edward I. that Sir Eustace de Hecche rode in the battle of Falkirk in 1298. It had a white stocking on its near hind leg, and according to one story its sire and grandsire had each a white stocking almost exactly similar.

Some say that this charger—it had several names, apparently—was killed in the battle, for it is known beyond dispute that many of the chargers owned by knights, barons, valets and esquires were slain in that great conflict.

Other reports, however, have it that Sir Eustace's mount came through the fight without a scratch. Sir Eustace was singularly attached to this particular horse and is said to have refused offers of large sums if he would sell it. He is also accredited with the remark that in courage and intelligence his bay charger eclipsed all other war horses he had ever owned.

Much of interest to do with horses has been narrated by a distinguished writer who flourished towards the end of the thirteenth and in the beginning of the fourteenth centuries —namely, Marco Polo. His remarks about the superstitions that were prevalent in his time are exceptionally instructive.

Writing of the city of Chandu which was founded by Kublai and that gave the name to the river known now as Shangtu, Polo tells us to remember that the Kaan owned an immense stud of white horses and mares, some 10,000 in all, "and not one with a speck or blemish visible." The milk of these mares was reserved for the Kaan and his family, "and they drank a great deal of it," the rest being given to some of the more distant relatives of the tribe.

Upon occasions, however, a tribe named Horiad was allowed to drink of the milk of the mares, "the privilege being granted them," as Polo says, "by Chinghas Kaan on account of a certain victory they long ago helped him to win."

Elsewhere Polo describes what may be termed the etiquette it was essential the traveller should observe who chanced to come upon the herd of white mares when they were travelling.

"Be he the greatest lord in the land," he tells us, "he must not presume to pass until the mares have gone by, but must either tarry where he is, or go half-a-day's journey round, if need so be, so as not to come nigh them, for they are to be treated with the greatest respect."

Non-observance of this unwritten law brought grief in its train, the punishments inflicted being as varied as they were horrible.

Furthermore, every year, on the 28th of August, "the lord set out from the park," upon which occasion none of the mares' milk was drunk. Instead it was collected in large-mouthed vessels kept expressly for the purpose and the occasion, and after that it was "sprinkled over a vast stretch of ground and in many different directions."

This was done "on the injunction of the Idolaters and Idol-priests," who steadfastly maintained that if the milk were thus sprinkled once a year "the Earth and the Air and the Gods shall have their share of it, and the Spirits likewise that inhabit the Air and the Earth.... And thus those beings will protect and bless the Kaan and his children, and his wives, and his folk, and his gear, and his cattle, and his horses, and his corn, and all that is his; and after this done the Emperor is off and away."

It is strange, also significant, that in almost every age allusion has been made to the respect habitually paid to white horses, especially pure white horses. From Homer we know that in his period, or towards the latter part of the eighth century B.C., the Thracians, the Illyrians and the people of Upper Europe spoke of white horses as though they almost worshipped them as gods.

In those early times it was deemed criminal intentionally to wound a white horse, while to kill one even by accident was thought to be but little less blameworthy—save, of course, upon occasions when a white horse was to be sacrificed to please the gods or to appease their anger.

Some centuries later Herodotus virtually repeats what Homer has already told us, and gives us to understand in addition that by that time parts of Russia teemed with white horses, many of them of great value.

Whether towards the end of the third and the beginning of the second centuries B.C. the Russians treated even white horses with ordinary humanity would appear doubtful, though we know that Russians entertained superstitious and grotesque beliefs concerning horses that were either white or cream-coloured.

Finally, some seven centuries later, Marco Polo comes with his remarkable narratives of the Tartars' herds of white horses and their strange beliefs concerning them. From other sources particulars may be obtained of the barbarous practices these Tartars had recourse to upon the occasions of their sacrificial ceremonies, particulars of too revolting a nature to be given here.

And now again we find allusion to the Turf. Apparently Edward II. disliked horse racing—such horse-racing as there was in his reign—and all that appertained to it, for upon the feast of St George in the year 1309 we find him interdicting "a tournament which was to be held on Newmarket Heath"; an act that made him unpopular for the moment, though when some years later he deliberately put a stop to preparations in progress in connection with a similar tournament nobody seemed much to mind.

That the people of England were none the less interested in horses at about this time we may infer from the knowledge we have that John Gyfford and William Twety had already issued their books upon horses and hunting, books to be seen to this day among the manuscripts in the Cottonian Collection, and that were, if one may express it so, widely read when first written.

Strictly dissimilar were the views of Edward III. from those of his predecessors where the subject of horses and the various forms of sport in which the horse plays a prominent part were concerned. The steps taken by Edward II.

deliberately to foster general dislike of certain branches of sport had not achieved the desired effect save amongst his small circle of sycophants, and one of Edward III.'s first acts upon succeeding him was to gather together a stud of the swiftest running horses procurable.

This act it was that led the popular King of Navarre to select "two swift-running horses of great beauty" from his stable and send them as a present to Edward III.; a compliment which pleased Edward greatly and that he quickly acknowledged.

In this reign, also in the reign of the succeeding monarch, Richard II., Acts were passed which directly tended to encourage the breeding and rearing of good horses. Indeed the sums spent by Edward III. in connection with this must have been prodigious, for it is on record that upon one occasion he purchased from the Count of Hainault alone horses to the value of some 25,000 florins.

Many of the horses that he bought, however, came direct from the Low Countries. Among the royal manors where he established large studs, especially studs of war horses, were Woodstock, Waltham, Odiham, and of course Windsor, a proportion of the expense of inaugurating and supporting these stud farms being defrayed by the sheriffs, according to royal command.

Yet, in spite of all this, the supply of horses obtainable was not equal to the demand when the great war with France broke out. At the battle of Crecy, in 1346, only a proportion of the army of Edward III. and the Black Prince had horses, though we know that almost on the eve of the campaign considerable sums were spent upon the purchase of horses from the King of Gascony and from several large owners.

This seems stranger still when we remember that the

English army at Crecy was limited to some 36,000 men only, whereas King Philip's forces numbered over 130,000.

Crecy, indeed, is one of the few historical battles in which the army that was the best mounted did not win the day; but then all historians admit that the bowmen the English brought into the field upon that occasion were probably among the best disciplined and the most expert that had ever before been seen in action.

On the other hand the horses of the opposing forces were not of the best. Many had hardly been trained at all to arms, and many more had been commandeered and hurried into the field almost at the eleventh hour. Some historians hold that Philip's army would have fared better had there been fewer men-at-arms in the fighting line, and it is possible that upon this single occasion if the army had had fewer horses it might have achieved success.

CHAPTER II

"WHEN the Pale was troubled by an eruption of the O'Byrnes and O'Moores in 1372" — Professor Ridgeway writes in his interesting and instructive work, "The Origin and Influence of the Thoroughbred Horse" — "who burned the priory of Athy, John Colton, the first Master of Gonville Hall (now Gonville and Caius College) and successively Dean of St Patrick's, Chancellor of Ireland, and Archbishop of Armagh, raised a force of twenty-six knights and a large body of men-at-arms and fell upon the Irish and defeated them with great slaughter."

Upon referring to the records of this incident, to be found in several of our histories, it becomes evident that in the Pale at that time there must have been many horses of the stamp that to-day we speak of as the "great" horse.

The insurrection alluded to so lightly as "an eruption of the O'Byrnes and O'Moores" in reality was a serious affair, due, we are told, mainly to the almost total disregard of certain just demands made by O'Byrne, O'Moore and their followers. The Irish were for the most part badly mounted and poorly armed, many of their horses having been seized surreptitiously a short time prior to the outbreak, but they

130

appear to have made a very gallant defence.

John Colton's men-at-arms were, however, nearly all of great weight and heavily armed, so it is not surprising to read that they "made short work of the Irish rebels." Remarkable would it have been had they not done so, for we must bear in mind that their suppressors were of immeasurably superior strength.

———————

A horse foaled some years after this, which lived to become famous in British history, was King Richard II.'s barbary, often called Roan Barbary. The king, we are told in rather extravagant language, "loved Roan Barbary as an only son," and certainly it is true that he was exceptionally fond of this particular horse which poets, dramatists and writers of romance at various periods have all united in immortalising.

Richard's grief and rage at hearing that Bolingbroke had chosen Roan Barbary, of all horses, upon which to ride to Westminster when he went there to be crowned, has many times been described, Shakespeare himself referring to the incident in *King Richard II.* in the well-known line, "When Bolingbroke rode on Roan Barbary, that horse that thou so often hast bestrid." Roan Barbary was a tall horse, well shaped and well schooled, but of uncertain temper. The king "could do with the steed whate'er he wished," but some of the grooms hardly dared approach to groom it "lest he sideways kick them."

It is interesting to note here that the history of early times, when it touches upon horses—which it does frequently—alludes upon many occasions to the partiality of particular horses for certain persons, and to their equally marked dislike for certain other persons.

The inference naturally would be that these particular horses were partial to the men who treated them humanely and disliked those who ill-treated them. If the early historians are to be believed, however, the horses' likes and dislikes for various persons were irrespective of the way they had been treated by such persons.

Particularly does this appear to have been the case with Roan Barbary, for we are assured that all who had charge of him, or to do with him in any way, treated him invariably "with kindness and great cordiality" (!) the king having issued strict orders that they should.

In the British Museum there may be seen to-day a French metrical history of the deposition of Richard II. which informs us that the king owned "many a good horse of foreign breed."

―――――――――

Mr J. P. Hore, the well-known authority, is of opinion that "the thoroughbred English horse was characteristic of the nation" in the reign of Richard II., and adds that "horses were then recognised and their praises sung."

There is no doubt that between 1377 and 1399 the interest taken in horses in this country by persons of almost every class developed rapidly. The agricultural community in particular had by then begun to turn its attention seriously to the rearing of a better stamp of horse, and we know that Chaucer, who lived from 1328 to 1400, tells us that his famous monk had "full many a daintie horse in stable."

Chaucer's interesting references to the various sorts of horse in use in the fourteenth century are numerous, and they serve to show that persons of different rank rode horses of different stamp. Thus on that fine April morning when the motley party of pilgrims set out from the Bell at Southwark upon their hasty journey we find the Knight mounted on a big and powerful horse—naturally a knight wearing armour needed such a beast to carry him—whereas the steed ridden by "the Clerk of Oxenford" was "as leane as any rake."

The Wife of Bath, on the other hand, with her "great spurs," sat astride an "amblere"; the Ploughman rode "a mere"; the Shipman from Dartmouth rode "a rouncy as he couth"; while the Reeve "sat upon a fit good stot that was all pomely gray, and highte Scot." In the "Knight's Tale" we find the King of Ynde riding "a horse of baye."

Apparently at this time greater attention was paid to the breeding and rearing of horses for war than for hunting or for "speed competitions" or any other purpose. Evidently King Richard had become more fully aware of the possibilities that existed for the use of powerful cavalry than any of his predecessors had done. Indeed he is said to have expressed upon one occasion a strong wish that his army might one day consist of cavalry only.

He believed, too, that the heavier the chargers were the more formidable the regiment must be, and so wholly did this belief obsess him that upon occasions he betrayed a tendency to overlook the fact that the heaviest horses in the world, the most finely trained—in short, the best—must necessarily prove comparatively useless unless their riders, in addition to being brave and well armed, were thoroughly trained horsemen and well disciplined.

Referring again to Chaucer, we find in the "Squire's Tale," which he did not finish, the well-known story of Cambuscan's wooden horse, and we find this also in "The

Arabian Nights"—that series of delightful narratives said to have been first made known by Antoine Gallard, the French Oriental scholar. The famous brazen horse of romance is the same, for it was Cambuscan's, and Cambuscan was King of Sarra, in Tartary. Cambuscan possessed, so it was said, all the virtues that are popularly attributed to a king, yet withal none of a king's vices; also he was said to be passionately devoted to his queen, Elfeta, who bore him two sons, Algarsife and Cambalo, and one daughter, Canace.

We are further told that the King of Arabia and India presented Cambuscan with "a steed of brass, which between sunrise and sunset would carry its rider to any spot on earth." To make the horse do this all that was necessary was that its rider should whisper into its ear the name of the place to which he wished to travel, and that he should then mount the horse and turn a pin set in its ear.

This done, the "animal" would go direct and at great speed to the place required, whereupon the rider turned another pin and descended. By turning a third pin it was possible to make the horse vanish and not reappear until its presence was again needed.

Aligero Clavileno was the full name of the winged horse with the wooden pin, the horse which Don Quixote rode upon the memorable occasion of his rescue of Dolorida and her companions.

But enough of fairy tales and nonsense. Coming to the subject of horse races in early times we find it gravely stated that "the earliest description of a horse race *per se* occurs in 1377," though we know that race meetings of a sort were held long before that date. The whereabouts of the track where the races in 1377 took place has not been ascertained, but it is known that some of the horses which ran belonged to Lord Arundel, and some to the Prince of Wales, so soon to become Richard II.

At this meeting it was that a match was arranged to take place between the Prince and Lord Arundel, each to ride his own animal. The match was run, and as the name of the winner has not, so far as I have been able to ascertain, been handed down to us, we may conclude that the Prince's horse was beaten. Had the winner been ridden by a Prince of Wales some record of the victory would assuredly be extant.

That Richard II. was a fine horseman, as finished horsemanship was understood in those days, there can be but little doubt. Yet it is remarkable that the natural gift known as "hands"—that is to say the power some men have of controlling a horse by delicate manipulation of the reins as opposed to brute force—apparently was not taken into consideration in the early centuries, or else was not understood and consequently not cultivated. To-day, of course, a man with bad "hands" is not deemed a horseman, properly speaking.

Thus it comes that we find some of the early instructors in horsemanship deliberately advising the novice to catch hold of the reins tightly in order to keep his seat with greater ease! Some of the early pictures, too, of men on horseback show the rider with his hands firmly clenched, even when the horse is walking, the reins held quite tight.

It has been argued that men sheathed from head to foot in the heavy plate armour of the fifteenth century could not have ridden gracefully even had they wished to do so. Long before armour of that pattern had come into vogue, however, the riders apparently were indifferent horsemen inasmuch as they had for the most part bad "hands," if we are to judge from early pictures and descriptions.

Many stories to do with horses have been woven round the celebrated French knight, Pierre du Terrail, Chevalier Bayard, and it is known that whatever the qualities, fictitious or otherwise, may have been that his horses are alleged to have possessed, Bayard was a fine rider, "the boldest horseman of his period" as one historian describes him.

Of medium height, slim, and a light weight, he was "of wholly irreproachable character"; hence the description which still clings to his memory—*Le chevalier sans peur et sans reproche.*

Truly remarkable are some of the feats of horsemanship attributed to him still. Thus it is said that he could ride any horse bareback and without a bridle, and that he rode in this way several savage animals which, when saddled and bridled, several famous horsemen were not able even to mount. But such stories must, of course, be believed only in part.

Probably the best horse owned by this knight was the one named Carman, or Carmen, a gift of the Duke of Lorrain. Particulars about its make and shape apparently are not on record, but Carman carried Bayard through several severe engagements, though thrice severely wounded.

It is said that Bayard was able to guide this horse by word of mouth alone, when he found it advisable to do so, and that upon some occasions the steed "would neigh in reply as though joyful at hearing its master's voice."

Furthermore he could ride Carman over country no matter how rough, and the horse would never slip or stumble. It may in addition have been a clever fencer, for we read that the knight "rode with reckless daring at many obstacles" when mounted on his favourite steed.

In at least one work of fiction the Chevalier Bayard has been rather amusingly confounded with the mythological steed of the four sons of Aymon that bore the name Bayard and that used so conveniently to grow larger when more than one of the four sons wanted to mount it at the same time. The name is said to signify the colour of bright bay, and the legend still obtains that a hoof mark of this mythical horse remains to this day in the forest of Soignes, while another of its hoof marks may be seen on a rock near Dinant. It was of this horse that Sir Walter Scott wrote in *The Lady of the Lake* the following lines:—

"Stand, Bayard, stand! The steed obeyed
With arching neck, and bended head,
And glaring eye and quivering ear,
As if he loved his lord to hear."

The Earl of Warwick's coal-black charger, Black Saladin, is eulogised in almost every history of the Wars of the Roses; yet, when all is said, Black Saladin does not appear to have done anything sufficiently remarkable to have justified his earning the immortal reputation that he undoubtedly has obtained. A big, powerful animal, it must in justice be said of him that he carried his master creditably through several rather bloody encounters before man and horse were killed in the great conflict at Barnet.

According to Hume's "History of England"—and probably no history extant is more accurate in detail—Warwick, when he received the fatal thrust, was fighting on foot.

No trustworthy description is obtainable of the horse that

Joan of Arc rode when she led the French army so successfully against the previously victorious troops of Henry VI. Only one indisputable statement relating to her leadership upon that famous occasion has been handed down to us, and that is that she rode astride.

Pictures innumerable have been painted that depict her as she is supposed to have appeared in the heat of the fray, and others that show her to us as she ought to have looked when the engagement was over. By basing our impressions solely upon such pictures we might well conclude that the Pucelle went into action riding a white horse; that in the thick of the fight she changed first on to a dun-coloured mare and then on to a bright bay mare; and that when the engagement was over she once more changed horses in order to ride back triumphant on a stallion as black as Black Saladin himself!

According to Mr Douglas Murray, whose "History of Joan of Arc," published recently, is the most exhaustive and authoritative work we have upon the career of that heroic young woman, Joan would appear to have been quite a good horsewoman. "She rode horses so ill-tempered that no one else would dare to mount them." The Duke of Lorraine, also the Duc d'Alençon, after seeing her skill in riding a course, each gave her a horse; and we read also of the gift of a war horse from the town of Orleans, and "many horses of value" sent from the Duke of Brittany. She had entered Orleans on a white horse, according to the *Journal du Siège d'Orleans*; but seems to have been in the habit of riding black chargers in war; and mention is also made by Chatelain of a "lyart" or grey.

A story, repeated in a letter from Guy de Laval, a grandson of Bertrand du Guesclin, relates that on one occasion when her horse, "a fine black war horse," was brought to the door, he was so restive that he would not stand still. "Take him to the Cross," she said; and there he stood, "as though he were tied," while she mounted. This was at Selles, in 1429.

Two famous horses of the fifteenth century were King Richard's White Surrey, and Savoy, the favourite steed of King Charles VIII. of France, which was coal-black and took its name from the Duke of Savoy from whom King Charles had received it as a present.

The king rode White Surrey frequently when travelling in state. That he had many other white steeds seems obvious, and evidently he was extremely partial to horses of that colour, for we find him telling his nobles to use their influence to induce the wealthier section of his subjects to breed and rear horses "white and grey."

Savoy, though what we should to-day term a "good plucked" horse, is said to have been "of mean stature," also it had a blind eye. Charles VIII. nevertheless rode it in preference to any other horse in his stud, and that his stud was a very large one we are told by some of the earlier historians.

Not a graceful horseman, he nevertheless had a firm seat, and it is interesting to read that he was extremely sensitive upon the subject of his horsemanship. So emphatically was this the case that upon one occasion he severely rebuked one of his courtiers who had remarked unwittingly in his presence that men existed who were physically incapable of becoming good riders. According to this king, indeed, one of the duties of every gentleman was to become proficient in the art of horsemanship.

At about this time—that is to say towards the close of the fifteenth century—a book that has since been rightly or wrongly described as "the first work on sport ever issued in England" was published. When first it appeared it attracted much attention. Printed for Dame Julyana Berners, who evidently had much practical knowledge of horses and the way to manage them, it mentions incidentally that every good horse ought to possess the following fifteen "properties": —

"Of a man: —bolde, prowde, and hardy.
Of a woman: —fayrbrested, fayr of heere, and easy to leape upon.
Of a fox: —a fayr taylle, short eeres, with a good
Of a haare: —a grete eye, a dry hede, and well runnynge.
Of an asse: —a bygge chyn, a flatte legge, and a good hoof."

From the above list we may conclude that in spite of the unwieldy appearance of most of the horses shown in the early drawings there must have been plenty of active animals in England long before the second half of the sixteenth century. Most likely the large and clumsy horses belonged practically to the class that to-day we speak of as shire horses, and that the majority were employed for carrying men in armour, historians being unanimous in declaring that by the middle of the sixteenth century a man of medium height could not, when sheathed in armour, have weighed together with the armour worn by his horse less than some thirty stone, and that often he must have weighed more.

This no doubt is the reason we read so frequently that in the sixteenth century considerable attention was paid to breeding and rearing great horses of Flanders, Friesland, France and Germany.

The majority of our historians seem not to have realised

fully that in Thomas Wolsey, afterwards Cardinal Wolsey, we had probably one of the finest horsemen of the period of Henry VII. and Henry VIII. The extreme brilliancy of Wolsey's public career possibly may have caused his lesser accomplishments to be eclipsed or over-looked, for that he possessed minor accomplishments is well known.

It was in Henry VII.'s reign, and probably about the year 1500, that Wolsey first had occasion to display his horsemanship in rather a prominent manner. For we read that "the king, having received a communication from the reigning emperor, Maximilian, and being at a loss as to how he should reply to it in the shortest possible time, turned abruptly to Thomas Wolsey to solicit his advice, Wolsey being at that time the king's chaplain; whereupon Wolsey replied without hesitation that if the king would entrust him with a despatch he would deliver it to the emperor with but little delay."

After pondering the proposal for some moments, Henry accepted the offer, and a little later handed to Wolsey a sealed packet, urging him to convey it with all speed and not be hindered by anybody. This took place, we are told, at Richmond, at about noon. Then and there the chaplain mounted the horse he had ready, and rode away.

That he must have galloped almost all the way to Dover, changing horses several times, is certain, for he arrived there on the following morning before daylight. By noon on the day after he was at Calais, and at nightfall he personally handed King Henry's sealed dispatch to to the Emperor Maximilian. Having received Maximilian's reply, Wolsey at once mounted a fresh horse that had been saddled for him and set out once more for Calais, which town he reached on the same night, so that by the following evening he was again at Richmond.

The king, however, had already retired to rest, and Wolsey therefore was compelled to wait until the morning to deliver Maximilian's reply. It so happened that he was walking in the park when presently the king overtook him and at once began to upbraid him for his delay in starting for France. Wolsey remained silent and collected until the king had stopped speaking, then, without a word, he produced the despatch that he had brought from Maximilian.

King Henry, we are told, was thereupon "both amazed and delighted," and with great rapidity the story of the chaplain's remarkable ride to Paris and back again was noised abroad.

Wolsey's reputation for horsemanship was firmly established from that time forward, and Henry, to mark his appreciation of the chaplain's exploit, bestowed upon him the deanery of Lincoln, and not long afterwards made him his almoner. Thus did the man obtain his first step to power who one day was to become the all-powerful Cardinal.

I have not been able to find in any books or documents particulars concerning the horses ridden by Wolsey in that famous journey. From what has been said, however, we may conclude that he rode horses of a stamp very different from the heavy, clumsy animals so plentiful in England at the time, for to have covered so many miles in so few hours the horses must have been of the swiftest, especially when it is remembered that the roads at that period were of the roughest possible description.

In later years, owing partly to his increasing weight, Wolsey almost entirely gave up riding. Yet the interest that he had always taken in horse breeding remained, and though his many and arduous duties occupied much of his leisure he nevertheless found time to devote some of his attention to the rearing of riding and driving horses, and to the breeding of shire horses.

Some of his Eastern sires, indeed—and we know that he had a large stud of them—are said to have been among the most valuable of the breeding stock that until then had ever been known, which may have been the reason that in after years Queen Elizabeth expended such vast sums upon increasing and still further improving the stud that had been Wolsey's.

Elizabeth, however, as we shall presently see, upon the whole took greater interest in "running horses" than in the clumsy shire stallions, and though it is said that she never was actually present at a race meeting held at Newmarket, she is known to have owned a number of race horses the majority of which were stabled near Greenwich and trained chiefly upon Blackheath.

In connection with Wolsey and his undoubted fondness for horses, it is interesting to learn that he cared but little for any form of gambling, though "the sight of a contest between running horses of high spirit delighted him." Until the period when he gave up riding he preferred at all times to be himself on horseback rather than watch others, a statement that has been misinterpreted by one writer to mean that Wolsey preferred to ride in races rather than watch others ride races for him!

I believe I am right in saying that Wolsey never rode in any race of any kind, also that he took more active interest in the chase than in the turf—such turf, that is to say, as there was in the fifteenth and sixteenth centuries to take interest in.

Upon that point Henry VII. held views somewhat different from his chaplain's. The spectacle afforded by a horse race gave him scant gratification, and as a result he did little to develop and encourage horse racing or to better the condition of the turf.

Probably the only ride in the nature of a horse race that did stir him into displaying enthusiasm was Wolsey's race just described. This feat Wolsey but rarely spoke about, save when questioned by friends. His technical knowledge of horses is said to have been profound, so much so that frequently men quite unknown to him would come many miles to obtain his opinion upon the condition of a sick horse, and usually he was willing to tender advice even to strangers.

Indeed his willingness to be of service when a horse was in distress appears to have remained one of Wolsey's marked characteristics until nearly the end of his life. Historians have for the most part depicted him a stern, unbending man from the time he was made Cardinal; yet he is known to have performed many small acts of kindness for which the world probably did not give him credit.

Whether the advice he tendered in cases of horse sickness was invariably sound is doubtful. The amazing ignorance of the anatomy of the human body that prevailed four hundred years ago leads naturally to the inference that ignorance of the anatomy of the horse must have been even greater. Probably the advice tendered by Wolsey was about upon a par in point of soundness with the advice that passed current towards the end of the fifteenth and the beginning of the sixteenth centuries for "wisdom in medicine and chirurgery."

Certainly we do not find allusion made to such common modern ailments in horses as spavins, navicular, ringbones and splints. Cracked heels may have been a common frequent source of lameness, for the shoes ordinarily used were clumsy, crude things knocked into shape in a rudimentary way, even those with which the most valuable of horses were commonly shod.

The horse breakers and trainers of the early part of the sixteenth century seem to have been of one opinion as to the most effectual way of, so to speak, bringing a horse to his senses, and that was the simplest way of all—namely, by starving him!

That so barbarous, and, let it be added so wholly ineffectual a method should have been resorted to where horses were concerned is perhaps hardly to be wondered at when we bear in mind that only a little over a century ago the same method was employed with lunatics who showed signs of insubordination.

For the idea used to be—and it has not yet quite died out—that a high temper must primarily be the outcome of high feeding. We read that upon one occasion Henry VII. commanded that a horse he was to ride in a public procession be left unfed for twenty-four hours, and as no reason is assigned for the order we are justified in conjecturing that he must have felt inwardly nervous, possibly that he feared the animal might, if fed as usual, prove to be what we call to-day "a handful"!

In other respects the horses of some four hundred years ago would seem to have been treated at any rate with ordinary humanity.

CHAPTER III

THE accession of Henry VIII. to the throne, in 1509, marked the beginning of a great development in the breeding and rearing of valuable horses, for that erratic monarch, whatever his failings may have been—and that he had a few failings we have reason to know—was at heart a sportsman in the true meaning of the now frequently misused term.

We read that soon after ascending the throne "he took steps to arrange for the importation from Italy, Spain, Turkey and elsewhere, at regular intervals, of the best stallions and some of the best mares procurable." That done, he set to work to establish at Hampton Court the Royal Stud which later was to become so famous, and among the many horses he received as gifts—the majority from men anxious to keep in favour with a monarch so all-powerful— were the famous mares "perfect in shape and size" that Francesco Gonzaga, the Marquis of Mantua, sent over in 1514, a gift to which he soon afterwards added "a Barb worth its weight in silver" which he declared he had taken great pains to secure.

That Henry was deeply gratified is obvious from his remark that he "had never ridden better trained horses," and that "for years he had not received such an agreeable present."

––––––––––––––––

As time went on, and the Royal Stud steadily increased, the fame of Henry's horses spread not only throughout the kingdom, but also across the seas and into remote parts of the Continent, with the natural result that presently attempts were made to obtain surreptitiously foals known to have been bred in the famous paddocks.

Henry, upon hearing this, became extremely angry, and this knowledge it probably was that in a measure prompted him to render illegal the exportation beyond the seas of mares or horses bred in England, and, in addition, to threaten with severe punishment anyone discovered making the attempt.

There cannot, indeed, be any doubt that before the passing of this Act many horses had been sent abroad from various parts of the country, and that in consequence the British stock probably would soon have depreciated in value had Henry not thus effectually put a stop to the practice at the outset.

Yet we are told that in spite of this the king's act greatly annoyed several of the more powerful of his nobles, even that in some of the provinces it led almost to open rebellion, many men of private means having been in the habit of considerably augmenting their fortunes by secretly exporting horses upon what was in those days deemed to be rather a large scale.

So strong, indeed, did the feeling throughout the country gradually grow, that in a short time it was decided to present the king with "a request"—presumably what we should to-day term a petition—in the hope that he might thereby be induced to revoke his rather arbitrary order.

Whether the request ever was presented does not appear, but certainly Henry did not revoke the order.

On the contrary, soon after prohibiting the exportation of horses beyond the seas he issued a supplementary edict which in effect rendered the exportation of horses to any foreign port, with the exception of Calais, a very grave offence; while the "exportation" of horses into Scotland, and even the bare act of selling to any Scotsman any horse without having first obtained the king's permission to do so, became an act of felony alike to vendor and purchaser.

Of course so unjust a law as the latter soon stirred up a strong feeling of resentment amongst Henry's subjects; yet in spite of their bitter complaints they were compelled to comply with it.

Thus it soon came about that men who had been living comparatively in opulence before the passing of these laws now found themselves reduced to genteel poverty, whereupon, as if to add insult to injury, Henry passed yet another statute—27, Henry VIII., c. 6.

This statute enacted that all farmers in receipt of a certain stated income, also all owners of parks, as well as certain other persons, should rear and keep a specified number of brood mares, of a height not less than thirteen hands, the penalty for failing to comply with the order being fixed at forty shillings a month.

The statute in addition commanded that upon every park of not less than four miles in extent—this is understood to have meant four miles in circumference—at least four mares should be kept, the same fine, forty shillings a month, to be extorted from all who failed to keep the law.

That these laws, though severe and unjust, achieved their purpose we may conclude from the statement that soon after they had been passed there were to be found in England five times more horses ready to be put into the field in a case of emergency, and that these horses were all of great value.

Yet once again an attempt was made to induce Henry to revoke his laws forbidding the exportation of horses, and again the attempt proved futile. The Scottish nation in particular felt deeply aggrieved at what they somewhat naturally deemed to be an insult paid to them by the king, but Henry, beyond threatening that if the complaints continued he would put a stop to them in rather a forcible manner, paid no heed whatever. And at just about this time it was that a number of Lowlanders were, so it is alleged, severely punished for purchasing horses of Englishmen in defiance of Henry's command.

And still the king remained unsatisfied. He had openly declared that he would transform England into the foremost country in Europe for valuable and well-bred horses, and to facilitate his doing so he presently passed another statute.

In this statute he commanded that stoned horses under fifteen hands were not to be put to pasture in any wood or forest in certain counties (which he mentioned), the penalty for breaking the law to be forfeiture to the Crown, while in certain other counties the law was to apply to horses under fourteen hands.

Yet another statute which he drew up—33, Henry VIII., c. 5—enacted that dukes and archbishops must maintain seven stoned trotting horses for the saddle; marquises, earls and bishops, five; and viscounts and barons with incomes of not less than 1000 marks, five.

In the same way subjects with an income of 500 marks

were each to maintain two of these trotting horses for the saddle, while men with an income of 100 marks, whose wives should "wear any gown of silk, or any French hood or bonnet of velvet, with any habiliment, paste or egg of gold, pearl or stone, or any chain of gold about their necks, or in their partlets, or in any apparel on their body," were by the law compelled to maintain one saddle horse, severe penalties being inflicted if they failed to do so.

I have somewhere seen it stated that these Acts were repealed by Edward VI., but they were not. They were developed by William and Mary, and further developed by Elizabeth. Upon each occasion the renewal and development of these statutes caused bad blood and brought forth threats of retaliation, but the latter were not carried out.

That the obvious injustice of laws so arbitrary should have created friction, is not to be wondered at; yet the benefit that subsequently accrued to the country through passing them was enormous.

Indeed it is more than likely that if Henry VIII., William and Mary, and Elizabeth had given way to the demands of a great body of their subjects between three and four hundred years ago, England would not have become famous above all other countries for its horses, as it is to-day.

It was in the reign of Henry VIII. that riding matches first began to acquire popularity, and to attract the attention of the "bloods" of about that period. Several descriptions of the way in which such matches were arranged and carried out are in existence, and perhaps a brief account of rather a famous match that was ridden by Richard de la Pole, the third Duke of Suffolk, against Seigneur Nicolle Dex, will here prove of interest.

The Duke of Suffolk—"Blanche Rose" as his intimate

friends called him—was the third son of John de la Pole, his mother being the Lady Elizabeth Plantagenet, Edward IV.'s and Richard III.'s sister.

In the year 1517, soon after the Duke had returned to Metz, the popularity of the turf began suddenly to increase, and thus it happened that the Duke presently became the possessor of a horse said to be "very swift and of extreme value," of which he boasted that it could beat all comers. It was while talking thus in Metz one day that Blanche Rose was taken at his word by the Seigneur Nicolle Dex, who declared without hesitation that he could and would himself produce and ride a horse against the Duke's "from the Elm at Avegney to within St Clement's Gate," for the sum of eighty crowns "and win easily."

At once Blanche Rose accepted the challenge, promising at the same time that he too would ride his own horse, and forthwith the stakes were handed to "an independent and neutral person" by each of the contestants.

Arrangements having been made that the match should be run early in the morning of St Clement's Day, May 2nd, we read that, "a ce jour meisme que l'on courre l'awaine et le baicon au dit lieu St Clement," the two riders, accompanied by many of their friends, went out through St Thiebault's gate, which had been opened before the usual time to suit their convenience, "and so passed into the field for the race."

There was much wagering on the result, and, as we should to-day express it, the Duke's mount was hot favourite. That Seigneur Nicolle was no novice in race riding is made manifest by the statement that he had taken the precaution to have his horse shod with extremely light shoes, also that "he came into the field like a groom, in his doublet and without shoes, and with no saddle but with a cloth tied round the horse's belly," whereas the Duke wore comparatively heavy clothing and rode in a heavy saddle.

The Duke's horse, however, jumped away with the lead and retained it during the first half of the race, "but when they were near St Laidre his horse lagged behind, so that the Duke urged him on with spurs until the blood streamed down on both sides; but it was in vain, Nicolle gained the race and the hundred and sixty crowns of the sum."

Several writers tell us that Nicolle Dex had trained his horse on white wine, but the truth would seem to be that he himself trained on white wine. We are informed, in addition, that the horse was not given any hay.

"Le dit Seigneur Nicolle n'avoit point donne de foin a son chevaulx, ne n'avoit beu aultre chose que du vin blanc."

What the horses of four hundred years ago were chiefly fed on is uncertain. We know that usually they were given hay, but we find mention made repeatedly of "horse bread." Probably this horse bread resembled the modern oil cake upon which cattle is fed, for we read that it tended to make the horses' coats "soft and glossy," an attribute of oil cake of which horse dealers are well aware.

It seems hardly necessary to mention in this connection that in Henry VIII.'s time, and indeed down to a much later period, the art of training horses, as we understand it to-day, was practically in its infancy. Also we are able to infer that it was quite a common practice to give a horse a drink of water just before running him in a race, and that what we to-day allude to as the art of judging pace in connection with race riding probably had never been even thought of.

In Henry VIII.'s reign the habit of naming horses after their breeder on their previous owner would appear to have come into vogue rather largely, and from that time onward, for some three centuries and a half, to have remained in vogue. After that it became customary to name race horses in rather a grotesque manner.

I have by me a list of names of race horses almost all of which must have been animals well known in their time. It would be interesting to hear what Messrs Weatherby would say if we asked them to-day to enter a mare to run under the name "Pretty Harlot" or, better still, "Sweetest when Naked"!

Among Henry VIII.'s famous barbs we find several mentioned by name, and we read incidentally that "during four or six days the king rode both Altobello and Governatore, but preferred Governatore."

The Marquis of Mantua had been renowned for his skill in horsemanship, as well as for the famous stud of horses that he possessed, for some years before Henry VIII. came to the throne, and this stud is said to have reached the acme of its excellence about the year 1517, when Gonzaga, as the Marquis was generally called, received many more requests for the service of his stallions than he was able to accede to.

Many, if not actually the majority of the horses that proved most successful upon the turf during the sixteenth century are said to have been descendants of the stock bred so carefully and with so much discrimination by Gonzaga or by King Henry, from which we may conclude that the assertion made often that until the reign of Queen Anne there were no race horses in this country worth speaking of is erroneous.

It is said, apparently with truth, that Gonzaga became extremely angry when, in the year 1515—only a few months after he had presented Henry with the valuable horses already referred to—Ferdinand of Arragon sent Henry "a gift of two most excellent horses," with the message that he,

Ferdinand, believed they would be found to outclass even the fine horses already in the royal stables at Hampton Court.

An apparently trivial incident such as this helps to show how thoroughly in earnest the men of fortune must have been who early in the sixteenth century devoted much time and attention to the breeding and rearing of valuable horses. It has been alleged that the Marquis of Mantua made his initial present of horses to King Henry solely in order to ingratiate himself in royal favour; but the anxiety he clearly displayed upon several occasions when gifts of horses were sent to Henry by men of rank and fortune leads to the belief either that Gonzaga must have been of a jealous nature, or else that he was inordinately proud of his own stud and extremely desirous that its high reputation should be maintained.

The value of the two horses sent over by Ferdinand is said to have been approximately 100,000 ducats. That would seem to be an impossible sum to have paid in a period when money was worth many times more than it is to-day; but when we read that both horses were richly caparisoned (*regio ornatu*) we may well suppose that the sum named included also the cost of trappings.

Under the circumstances it is perhaps not surprising that Ferdinand of Arragon—Ferdinand the Catholic, as he was popularly called—should have been deemed insane by a great body of his subjects when it became known that he had sent so extravagant a gift to King Henry, his son-in-law.

So prevalent, indeed, was this impression, that reasons were at once put forward to account for the alleged lack of intellect. Thus the incident of his having been poisoned two years before by his new queen, Germaine de Fois, was mentioned amongst possible causes, the serious illness that

155

followed having proved almost fatal.

Particulars of this attempt upon the life of Ferdinand the Catholic are to be found in one of the letters of Peter Martyr, though the writer of the letter does not seem to think that any insanity with which the king may have been afflicted towards the close of his life can have been due to the cause assigned. Indeed in one of these letters he directly attributes the king's death to over-indulgence in hunting and matrimony, either of which, as he says, is liable to hasten dissolution in a man over sixty years of age!

Not content with the very large and valuable stud that he now possessed, Henry found it necessary in 1518 to send "a Bolognese gentleman" out to Italy to choose still more horses for him there, special instructions being given to him that the best animals he could find in Italy must be bought at once, irrespective of cost, and shipped across to England without undue delay—an order that the Bolognese gentleman "obeyed implicitly and to the king's great satisfaction as well as to his own." There may well be a hidden meaning in the last words!

We do not hear anything more that is of interest and that has to do with Henry's stud until the year 1526, when we read that "eighteen of the finest of his horses were sent by King Henry VIII. as a gift to Francis I." The reason he sent so many is not stated, nor are we told if these were chargers, race horses or great horses.

After that the sending of gift horses apparently became an established custom amongst men of rank and of wealth, as well as amongst potentates, so much so that persons of quality vied one with another in sending gifts of valuable horses to their friends.

The last present of the sort received by Henry VIII.

consisted of twenty-five Spanish horses sent to him by the emperor, Charles V., in 1539.

Hunting is known to have been one of Henry's favourite amusements, and in a despatch dated 10th September 1519, written by Giustinian when Venetian Ambassador to England, we are informed that when Henry hunted he invariably rode several horses, or, in the words of the despatch, "never took that diversion without tiring eight or ten horses, which he caused to be stationed beforehand along the line of country he meant to take."

From this and similar statements it has been inferred that the hounds Henry hunted with ran some artificial line, that otherwise the horses could not have been stationed "beforehand along the line of country he meant to take." The probability, however, is that the king's horses were stationed at different points all over the country to be hunted, for it seems impossible that the king, heavy man though he undoubtedly was, could alone have ridden eight or ten horses to a standstill in a single day's hunting!

Indeed in Henry III.'s reign the men who hunted regularly most likely rode more than one horse a day, just as most hunting men do now. At that period the sport was, of course, very different from our modern foxhunting, and from the descriptions of it that have been handed down to us there is reason to believe that plenty of Henry's nobles hunted not because they were fond of the sport, but because they deemed it diplomatic to appear to be wholeheartedly as devoted to the chase as the king himself most certainly was.

Yet the king apparently was not hoodwinked as easily as he may have appeared to be, or feigned to be, for upon more than one occasion he availed himself of opportunities to make some of his sycophants look remarkably ridiculous in public.

In this connection an interesting little story is narrated of Sir Miles Partridge, a knight who figured rather largely in Henry VIII.'s reign. Apparently Sir Miles had more than once writhed in silence beneath the king's gibes, though all the while impatiently awaiting an opportunity to retaliate in a dignified way.

The opportunity came at last, when the king, in a merry mood, suggested to the knight that he should dice with him. This happened at about the time when the monasteries were being dissolved, and Henry's coffers were in consequence unusually well replenished. At first the king won persistently; then suddenly his luck deserted him, with the result that in the end he lost control of his temper and with an oath shouted at Sir Miles that he would stake upon a single throw of the dice the great bells of St Paul's against a hundred sovereigns.

The dice were thrown, and Sir Miles won, and the bells, described by a chronicler of the period as "the greatest peal in England," were taken away and melted down, to the knight's unfeigned delight.

It is said that the king never forgave Sir Miles Partridge for this. Later Sir Miles was charged with some criminal offence and imprisoned, and in 1551 he was beheaded on Tower Hill.

In the fifteenth and sixteenth centuries the horse continued to figure largely in romance, and thus it comes that we find horses, fictitious and otherwise, playing important rôles in the works of fiction of the principal authors of about that period.

Ariosto's immortal narrative of "Orlando Furioso," written towards the close of the fifteenth or in the beginning of the sixteenth century, has given us "the little vigilant horse," Vegliantio, called Veillantif in the French romance, where Orlando appears as Ronald.

Then we have "the horse of the golden bridle," Orlando's remarkable charger, Brigliadoro, whose speed equalled Bajardo's; also Sacripant's steed, Frontaletto, "the horse with the little head," that was capable of doing many extraordinary things. Sacripant, who was King of Circassia, and a Saracen, held secret consultations with Frontaletto, and the horse could understand its master's every word.

Rinaldo's horse, Bajardo, made famous in Ariosto's celebrated book, was a bright bay and very fast, and at one time it had belonged to Amadis of Gaul. When Malagigi, the wizard, found it in the cave guarded by "a dragon of great size," he at once, at considerable personal risk, attacked the dragon, which in the end he succeeded in slaying.

According to the legend, Bajardo is still alive, but under no circumstances can man approach it, nor will any man ever do so. Though Bajardo figures in several stories, it occurs first in "Orlando Furioso."

The original of Rinaldo was the son of the fourth Marquis d'Este, and Malagigi was Rinaldo's cousin. The habit of drawing fictitious characters to resemble closely living persons, or well-known persons of a previous period, was very prevalent among the writers of the sixteenth century, and therefore it often is difficult to disassociate the real from the fictitious character.

This may be said too of the horses that we come upon in some of the better-known of the old-world romances.

Indeed in several stories that could be named, the famous chargers of notable princes can be recognised under several assumed names.

With the close of Henry VIII.'s reign—that is, in 1547—we come to an end of what was without doubt a period in which the horse played a more conspicuous part than it had done since the Norman Conquest. Upon ascending the throne Henry had found the condition of horse breeding in this country in rather a bad way. With others, as we have seen, he had set to work in earnest to improve, to the best of his ability, the breed of English horses, and though some of the statutes that he enacted—also some of the methods to which he had recourse in order to accomplish his object—undoubtedly were drastic, directly and indirectly they helped to bring about the improvement he desired, and for this the nation still owes him a debt of gratitude.

Henry's fondness for the chase was equalled only by the keen interest he took in the rather primitive horse racing of his period, and trustworthy chroniclers tell us that one of his most cherished ambitions was to see established in England a stud of the fastest horses the world had ever known.

When we bear in mind his fondness for horses of all kinds it seems strange that he should not have been a first-rate judge of a horse. Of knowledge of a horse's anatomy he had practically none, for which reason his ignorance in this respect has been contrasted with the knowledge that Wolsey possessed. Once, indeed, when taxed with ignorance upon this point by one of his nobles he laughed heartily and admitted the impeachment.

The order, already referred to, that horses should not be sent across the border, or sold to Scotsmen, almost completely crippled the horse-breeding industry north of the Tweed. True, some of the more powerful of the Scottish clans still owned valuable breeding stock, yet so strictly were Henry's laws enforced that the chiefs even of those clans were, with but few exceptions, unable to buy English stallions or to obtain their services at any time during Henry's reign.

As a well-known Scottish historian has aptly put it, "Henry VIII. practically ruined Scotland so far as that country's prosperity had to do with the rearing of horses for the field, an unfair form of oppression that many Highlanders, and also Lowlanders, have not yet quite forgotten."

Perhaps it is worth mentioning here that so far as we are able to judge from the records of the early historians the men of Scotland have not, as a body, ever proved themselves to be such finished horsemen as the English, and more especially the Irish.

This statement is not made in the least in a captious spirit. Why should it be? Probably the reason the Scotch are, as a nation, less finished horsemen, is that they are men of large bone, considerable weight and great physical strength.

Historical records serve to show that no race of men so built ever has been particularly famous for finished horsemanship. For a man to be a finished horseman need not necessarily possess great physical strength, and the man of heavy build almost invariably finds himself at a disadvantage when on horseback by comparison with the man of spare frame, small bone and "flat" thighs. Though this is something of a truism, several of our early historians apparently forgot it.

A study of the world's history makes it clear that the tribes, races and nations especially renowned for their horsemanship have been composed for the most part of men of small stature.

CHAPTER IV

THE continent whose history and progress have been the least influenced by horses probably is Northern America, for it seems beyond doubt that when Columbus discovered it horses were unknown there.

How then did they come to be there in such immense herds in later years?

This question has been asked many times, and the reply generally is that the horses subsequently introduced there by the Spaniards must have bred with great rapidity.

Other solutions to the problem that have been put forward are hardly worth considering seriously. So enormous did these herds become, however, that down to half-a-century or so ago horses in their thousands ran wild over the vast prairies of the western states. At the present day such herds are practically extinct.

We read that when, in 1519, the renowned Hernando Cortes set out from Cuba to conquer the empire of Montezuma, he took with him "sixteen strong and picked horses." Bernal Diaz, who was Cortes' comrade, apparently was greatly devoted to horses, and in his famous account of the Conquest of Mexico he describes in detail each of these sixteen animals, and mentions in rather a quaint way the principal characteristic that each possessed.

Seeing that Cortes' force consisted of some 660 trained men and about 200 Indians, the sixteen horses of course in no way approached the number he would have liked to take, and the reason he took so few is made clear by Diaz when he tells us that owing to the smallness of the ships of that period and the limited amount of accommodation that could be found on board them, even in proportion to their size, the difficulty of transport was very great.

It was, indeed, owing chiefly to the difficulty of transporting horses to Cuba and Hispaniola from Spain that the prices demanded even for horses of inconsiderable value were so exorbitant. Even it seems possible that this scarcity of horses directly led to a campaign that was expected to last for only a few months being prolonged to approximately two years; for though Cortes set sail with his little army in February, 1519, the subjugation of Mexico was not completed until nearly two years had elapsed.

There seems to be no doubt but that the redoubtable Francisco Pizarro, who afterwards conquered so effectually the kingdom of the Incas, was in Hispaniola as early as the year 1510, and he may have been there even before that date. When, in 1524, he began to move southward from Panama on his famous expedition, he travelled without horses, and the attempt to reach the realm of gold proved futile.

His second expedition, however, was more successful, but then he had with him a number of horses that he had taken the precaution to buy before leaving Panama, and the expedition numbered, all told, about 160 men. The horses would appear to have been of the roughest, and some of them in poor condition, yet Pizarro positively refused to give leave for any of them to be destroyed, having apparently taken to heart the lesson he had received from the reverse which had overtaken him on his previous expedition when he was without horses.

It is probable, however, that even Pizarro was not prepared for the extraordinary part that was presently to be played by those very animals that he had with him.

For before he had advanced very far it became apparent to him that the native Indians had never in their lives before set eyes upon a horse, and thus it happened that when presently they beheld Pizarro's advancing cavaliers, their attitude, which until then had been both threatening and defensive, became almost immediately changed to one of terror.

Pizarro was at first amazed at this. Then as the Indians suddenly and of one accord turned and fled, uttering, as we are told, "strange and shrill cries," the truth flashed in upon him—his mounted men had been mistaken by them for some kind of weird creature, possibly something in the nature of a centaur!

As one writer says, "consternation seized the Indians when they saw a cavalier fall from his horse, for they were not prepared for the division into two parts of a creature that had seemed to them to be but a single being."

In a letter addressed to Henry Bullinger by Bishop Hooper there is a statement to the effect that "two most beautiful Spanish horses" were received by Edward VI. from the emperor, Charles V., on 26th March, 1550, and that the king expressed his delight at the gift by giving way to "extravagant conduct."

The incident is of interest because poor young Edward VI. was not supposed to be fond of horses. Yet Camden, the famous antiquary, who lived between 1551 and 1623 and was in a position that should have enabled him to speak with authority, gives it as his opinion that the lad took interest in horses of all kinds.

Hargrove, in his "History and Description of the ancient City of York," maintains that the origin of horse racing can be traced back "even to the time of the Romans," a statement apt to prove misleading if we take it quite literally.

That horse racing of a sort can be traced back to a very remote period has already been indicated, but, as we have also seen, almost the only kind of racing in which the Romans took keen interest was chariot racing, so there is reason to believe that some of the early allusions to chariot races may unwittingly have been confused with horse races by some of our later historians.

In a letter that appeared recently in a newspaper published in Ireland, and that dealt at length with the supposed origin of horse racing, the writer remarked with unconscious humour that "undoubtedly the first races in England were held in Scotland."

In this belief he was, of course, mistaken, though it is known that the Scottish people have from very early times been fond of horse racing, and that the great race meeting held in Haddington in 1552 attracted an enormous concourse of spectators from the Highlands and Lowlands alike.

Later the Haddington race meeting came to be held annually, the principal prize run for being "a silver bell of value."

Rather an eccentric individual, named David Hume, was

connected with the Turf in Scotland about the middle of the sixteenth century. He appears, indeed, to have been quite an interesting personality. A resident of Wedderburn, where he died in or about the year 1575—the early writers, while admitting that when he died he must have been fully fifty years of age, yet disagree as to the exact date of his death— he is especially worthy of mention because probably he was typical of a particular stamp of man that during the latter half of the sixteenth century was in a great measure responsible for the development of the race horse.

Presumably David Hume owned property, for he is spoken of as "a gentleman of good status in Berwickshire," and in later years his son, known as David Hume of Godscroft, wrote a book which became famous in Scottish literature, the "History of the House of Douglas."

The elder Hume is described as "a man remarkable for piety, probity, candour and integrity." How ironical that description unconsciously was we shall see in a moment. The son, we are told, "seldom missed an opportunity of speaking in still more laudatory terms of his father," but Mr J. P. Hore's opinion is to the effect that if some such institution as the modern Jockey Club had been in existence when Hume the elder was in his heyday, that gentleman would, in spite of his alleged probity, integrity, and so forth, have been warned off the Turf at short notice.

For we read that "so great a master in the art of riding was he that he would often be beat to-day and within eight days lay a double wager on the same horses and come off conqueror" (sic). No doubt this paragon of honour has many emulators on the Turf to-day, but the relatives and friends of the latter at least have not the effrontery to tell us that such men are "strictly just, utterly detesting all manner of fraud," the statement made again and again about the elder Hume by his kinsfolk.

Elsewhere we learn that sometimes he ran two horses in one race and that upon occasions he was able to hoodwink the spectators assembled into believing that a horse had tried hard to win when in reality it had barely extended itself.

Hume himself would talk openly to his friends about the races he meant to win, and apparently he seldom attempted to conceal the fact that some of his horses were meant to lose.

Possibly this very "ingenuousness" may have led some of his friends, and a proportion of what we should to-day call the general public, to believe that he acted honourably and always in good faith.

In justice let it be said, however, that he bred good stock, also that he was a better judge of a horse than the bulk of his contemporaries—though that is not high praise. While himself engaged in roguery in connection with racing he was all the time striving to purify the Turf. He would, in all probability, have amassed a large fortune—or what was deemed in those days to be a large fortune—had he been less addicted to gambling for gambling's sake, for it is certain that from first to last he won much money by laying against his own horses as well as by backing some of them. The more amazing, therefore, is it that certain writers, even in comparatively recent times, should speak of him in all seriousness as a man of remarkable integrity.

Queen Elizabeth loved the Turf and apparently was extremely fond of horses, while in her youth she must have been rather a fine horsewoman. She kept many riding horses for her own use and many more for the ladies of her court, and we know that she was extremely partial to chestnut animals.

There is not, I think, any trustworthy evidence that she ever attended a race meeting held at Newmarket, but the statement made in at least one history of her period that she witnessed races at Doncaster probably is accurate, for we have proofs that a racecourse had been laid down there or marked out by the year 1600. Also we know that Elizabeth was fond of gambling and that she squandered vast sums probably in connection with the turf.

It must be remembered, however, that in the second half of the sixteenth century gambling was a besetting vice. "In the reign of Queen Elizabeth," Mr Clarkson writes, "racing was carried on to such an excess as to injure the fortunes of many individuals, private matches being then made between gentlemen, who were generally their own jockeys and tryers."

The descriptions of some of these matches are almost as quaint as the account already given of the race between Blanche Rose and Nicolle Dex, for the majority of the riders were wont to have recourse to the worst sort of trickery when they believed it might enable them to win.

Thus an instance is recorded of ground glass being mixed with a mare's food, the ill-starred animal being in consequence hardly able to cover the course, on which she died in great agony when the race was over.

This statement is made without comment, and cases somewhat similar are cited which, if they occurred now, would fire our indignation and lead swiftly to retribution.

From this we may to some extent infer that the morality of the Turf in Queen Elizabeth's reign had sunk to a low ebb. Indeed the maxim the majority of the "tryers," even of the "gentleman tryers," apparently was—"Win honestly if possible—but win."

In Elizabeth's reign it was not customary to run important races for cups. Nearly all the "big" races were for "specie," or else for a silver bell—sometimes for both. Silver bells awarded as prizes over three hundred years ago are, it is said, still to be seen in some old country houses and in some museums, but though I have tried I have not been able to discover the whereabouts of any of them.

In 1603 the Earl of Essex offered a snaffle made of gold as a prize to be run for at a race meeting held near Salisbury, and at about the same time it was proposed that "race gatherings" should take place near Salisbury at fixed intervals.

The latter suggestion, though strongly resented by "a number of Salisbury gentlemen" who presumably were under the impression that to establish a race course near their town must necessarily prove demoralising to the townsmen, was eventually adopted, the queen having, so it was said, brought her influence to bear in favour of the proposal.

We may approximately estimate the value of horses of a particular stamp at about this time from an inventory that was drawn up in 1572 of the effects of the second Earl of Cumberland of Skipton Castle.

Therein we find a stoned horse called Young Mark Antony valued at £16; another horse, Grey Clyfford, at £11: Whyte Dacre, at £10; Sorrell Tempest, £4; White Tempest and Baye Tempest, each at £5; Baye Myddleton, £1, and so on. Some mares and their followers are also mentioned, and lastly ten cart horses.

Many fictitious stories have been woven around Suleiman, the favourite charger of the Earl of Essex, but they are not of sufficient interest to place on record. In Elizabeth's reign a number of barbs, also many Spanish horses descended from barbs, were obtained from captured foreign vessels, and these the queen looked upon for the most part as her personal perquisites.

Consequently about the middle of her reign an order was issued that all captured horses must without exception be sent direct to the queen, the infliction of a severe penalty being threatened if the order should be disregarded. A number of these animals were subsequently sent as gifts to the more faithful of her nobles, and all the recipients sent in return "expressions of extremest gratitude."

There is a diversity of opinion as to what constituted "the staple article of food" of horses in the sixteenth century, though of course hay was used largely. Bishop Hall throws some light upon the subject when he mentions that thoroughbred stallions when largely in demand were given eggs and oysters.

Reference to eggs and oysters in this connection is made elsewhere, so we may conclude that the custom of thus feeding stallions was not an uncommon one, at any rate in the time of Elizabeth.

Horse bread has already been mentioned, but I have not come upon any direct allusion to oats being used to feed horses upon at this period.

Several of the writers in Elizabeth's reign openly bemoaned the development of horse racing, urging that trouble and disaster followed in its train, but their moans were for the most part stifled in the clamour of general approbation.

Among those who spoke strongly in condemnation of horse racing was the rather eccentric Lord Herbert of

Cherbury. Late in life he wrote—to the amusement of his friends and relatives—a complete history of his own career, in which volume he again reverts to his pet aversion by declaring that among the exercises of which he disapproved were "the riding of running horses, there being much cheating in that kind."

Hunting also he clearly objected to, for he goes on to tell his readers that he does not like hunting horses, "that exercise taking up more time than can be spared for a man studious to get knowledge."

From other of his remarks it becomes obvious that some three centuries ago the men who devoted the better part of their lives to the sport of hunting became to such a degree engrossed in it that in time they could hardly be brought to talk, or indeed to think, of anything else whatever.

That the same can be said with truth of a proportion of our modern hunting men is well known, and the question is asked to-day, as it was asked three hundred or more years ago—How comes it that over-indulgence in the chase has this odd effect upon us, whereas over-indulgence in other forms of sport but seldom makes its votaries shallow-minded to the same degree?

Indeed Lord Herbert of Cherbury, eccentric as he admittedly was, made many sensible observations upon this and kindred topics; and there can be no doubt that in decrying the then increasing tendency of men and women of what were looked upon as the educated classes to squander their fortunes, he voiced the views held by a vast proportion of the thinking population of this country.

A contemporary of Lord Herbert's wrote practically to the same effect. His name was Burton, and he reached his heyday about the time that Shakespeare's era was drawing to a close. The diatribe he launched against the increasing spread of gambling upon the Turf has probably never been surpassed in vigour.

In one of his mildest passages he pronounces horse races to be "the disport of great men, and good in themselves, though many gentlemen by such means gallop quite out of their fortunes."

Shakespeare himself, though rather fond of horses, was hardly less opposed to the practice of heavy betting. His description of a thoroughbred's points is good:

> "Round-hoof'd, short-jointed, fetlocks shag and long,
> Broad breast, full eye, small head, and nostrils wide,
> High crest, short ears, straight legs, and passing strong,
> Thin mane, thick tail, broad buttock, tender hide."

It would take long, also it is unnecessary, to describe at length all the horses of which Shakespeare speaks in his plays. According to a recent writer, Oliver's steed, Ferrant d'Espagne, or "Spanish traveller," has been "bastardised." What the writer means is, I think, that the horse has been introduced into works of fiction without acknowledgment.

Such certainly is the case, and so greatly has the animal been distorted in some instances that only with difficulty is it recognisable.

In Shakespeare's time—that is to say during the latter half of the sixteenth and in the beginning of the seventeenth centuries—the barbary horse clearly was highly esteemed, for it is referred to frequently in books and memoirs which bear upon that period.

Shakespeare speaks several times of roan horses too, as for instance in *I Henry IV.*, where we come upon the sentence, "Give the roan horse a drench." To bay horses he makes allusion in *King Lear*, in *Timon*, and elsewhere, and in *Timon* he refers also to a team of white horses. These bare allusions make dry reading, but they are instructive and of interest in connection with the story of the part the horse played in British history.

More especially is this so when we again bear in mind what has already been stated at length in the introductory note to this book, and that is the enormous extent to which automobilism has increased in this country, and for that matter the world over, since the introduction of the petrol motor, which makes it obvious that the horse's reign must be fast drawing to a close.

―――――――

That we have, as a nation, already to a great extent lost much of the interest we took only a few years ago in horses, and in all that appertains to them, is, I think, beyond dispute. The number of men who keep what must be termed "pleasure" horses decreases year by year, almost month by month, and indeed it would be possible to name at off-hand between fifty and sixty well-known men and women fond of sport who, within the last six months or so, have sold their carriages and all their harness horses, and whose stables now contain only hunters, while in other cases even the hunters have been got rid of in order to make way for automobiles.

And yet, bemoan the change though we may, the gradual transition is not uninteresting to study. History in the past has for centuries been both directly and indirectly affected by the horses and horsemanship of the various races the world over. History in the future is going to be similarly affected by motor power applied in a variety of ways.

And yet, who knows? Perhaps even half-a-century hence, when the horse will to all intents be extinct in England, save where he is kept for racing and in some instances for hunting purposes, interest may still be taken in Shakespeare's plays and therefore in the stories of such whimsical characters as the self-satisfied, conceited and generally grotesque Sir Andrew Aguecheek and his celebrated grey steed, Capilet, that we find portrayed so admirably in *Twelfth Night*; in Lord Lafeu of *All's Well that Ends Well* and his curious bay horse, Curtal, a name that means literally "the cropped one"; and in Cut, the carrier's horse of *King Henry IV.*,—to name but a few of Shakespeare's creations that surely must live on for ever.

With regard to barb horses, of which so much has been said and written, the probability would seem to be that "barbed" is in reality a corrupt form of the word "barded" that came originally from the French, *bardé*—that is to say, caparisoned—and therefore it may signify indirectly a horse in armour. Hence the meaning probably intended by Shakespeare to be conveyed in the following lines in *King Richard III.*:—

> "And now—instead of mounting barbed steeds,
> To fright the souls of fearful adversaries,—
> He capers nimbly in a lady's chamber,
> To the lascivious pleasing of a lute."

Shakespeare and Bishop Hall, in addition to one or two other writers, speak of the horse, Marocco, which lived in Elizabeth's reign, and belonged to a man named Banks, or Bankes, a brother of the first keeper of the New Warren.

Foaled, so far as one can gather, at Newmarket, Marocco appears to have been one of the cleverest of the few horses that at that period had been trained to perform at fairs, and in shows and circuses.

Some of the feats performed by it are described at length in the old records, and though we read that in those days such feats were deemed "marvellous past belief," we should smile if anybody were to-day to express amazement at seeing a circus horse perform tricks so simple.

That Marocco should be able to walk upright upon his hind legs, for instance, was considered so astounding that questions were asked in all seriousness as to whether supernatural aid of some kind had not been invoked!

In addition to this, Marocco would rear, kneel, sit, or lie down, when told to do so, and he would indicate amongst the spectators any individual selected by his trainer.

What was deemed most remarkable of all, however, was a performance in which Marocco walked backwards, "the while turning in circles," when Banks ordered him to do so.

We are told that upon witnessing this performance a proportion of the audience was so deeply affected that several people dared not remain. Consequently one is less surprised at reading that when, later, Banks and his pupil gave a performance in Rome, both man and horse were pronounced to be in league with the devil and ordered to be publicly burnt as magicians, which monstrous sentence was duly carried out.

In justice let it be said that this act of barbarity—the direct outcome of the pitiable ignorance of the age—created intense indignation in England, while in Italy it stirred up a strong feeling of resentment.

Attempts were made later to create the impression that political wirepullers had been at work, and that man and horse had been sacrificed expressly to make bad blood between the British Court and the Vatican, if not between England and Italy, but there is no reason for believing that the agitators achieved their purpose.

Nor, indeed, is it certain that Banks' death sentence was pronounced by the Pope, or by his order. That the man had come to be looked upon as a magician, however, in every part of Italy where his horse had been exhibited, apparently is beyond dispute.

Though strolling players of many sorts were, as we know, plentiful in Elizabeth's reign, it seems more than likely that the exhibition given by Marocco may directly have inaugurated in England the practice of training animals to perform tricks of the same sort for public shows.

Certainly we hear soon after Marocco's tragic end that exhibitions of performing animals were advertised to take place in different parts of the country, and from that time onward incidental allusions to entertainments of the kind that we to-day call circuses are to be found in some of the old books.

There mention is made of the methods employed in order to train the animals to their owners' satisfaction, methods barbarous enough, in all conscience. Yet none took exception to them. For the tendency of the age, three centuries ago, and down probably to a much later period, was one of cruelty. The literature of the last three hundred years makes that but too apparent.

CHAPTER V

SO far as hunting was concerned, Henry VIII. was, as we know, a keen sportsman, and Queen Elizabeth would appear to have been almost an equally enthusiastic sportsman. Passionately devoted to the chase, nothing gave her greater pleasure than to see "the quarry broken up before her." Statements to this effect are to be found in the works of three trustworthy writers at least, so we may take it that the records are approximately accurate. The queen "loved to be on horseback for its own sake," and was fond of open air at all times.

It is in connection with Elizabeth's partiality for the chase that the story is told of a man named John Selwyn, for many years under keeper of the park at Oaklands, in Surrey, where some of the queen's hunters were usually stabled during the autumn and winter.

Selwyn must in several ways have been a remarkable character, but it is with his horsemanship only that we have here to deal. On the occasion, then, of a great stag hunt which the queen had arranged should take place in the park at Oaklands, Selwyn was "chief in attendance"—in other words, huntsman.

Suddenly, as we are told, a stag was started.

When it had been hunted only a short time, a fear was expressed by the queen that it would escape, "the animal having proved of such unusual swiftness that it was feared the hounds would not be able to overtake it."

Determined that this should not happen, "Selwyn pressed spurs to his horse, and galloping at an angle, and sideways," succeeded in coming alongside the stag as it was about to turn off abruptly.

At once the enthusiasm and excitement of the spectators, especially of the queen, became intense; nor did it abate when they saw Selwyn, still galloping at top speed, neck and neck with the stag, suddenly vault right off his horse's back on to the stag's, "where he kept his seat gracefully in spite of every effort of the affrighted beast to throw him off."

Thus he galloped on for some yards, the queen and all the spectators wondering what he would do next. They were not kept long in suspense. Of a sudden Selwyn swiftly but calmly drew out his hunting knife. Then he began to prod the animal with its point, first on one side of its neck, then on the other, until at last he succeeded in forcing the stag to gallop round to a point within a few yards of the very spot where the queen sat waiting.

At last, when the animal was very near the queen, its rider suddenly plunged his knife deep into its throat, "so that the blood spurted out and the beast fell dead just by her feet."

This display is said to have delighted the queen so greatly that she soon afterwards granted Selwyn several favours, and on the monument still to be seen at Walton-on-Thames he is portrayed in the act of stabbing, in the manner described, the stag slaughtered on that memorable occasion. Selwyn died on 27th March, 1587.

———————

Of the famous horses of fiction and romance in the sixteenth and seventeenth centuries, one or two more must be mentioned. Don Quixote's immortal squire, Sancho Panza, who, it will be remembered, rode upon an ass named Dapple, was Governor of Barataria.

Though endowed with common sense, and though his proverbs have become historical, he was wholly devoid of what is sometimes called "spirituality."

Nevertheless Don Quixote and his horse, Rosinante—a name that means literally "formerly a hack"—came gradually to be renowned the world over.

To this day, indeed, "a perfect Rosinante" is the comment not infrequently passed upon a horse that is mostly skin and bone.

Peter of Provence's wooden horse, Babieca, is another "creature" whose name must not be omitted.

"This very day," we read in Don Quixote, "may be seen in the King's armoury the identical peg with which Peter of Provence turned his wooden horse which carried him through the air. It is rather bigger than the pole of a coach, and stands near Babieca's saddle."

Don Quixote himself rode astride the wooden horse, Clavileno, on the occasion when he wished to disenchant the Infanta Antonomasia and her husband shut up in the tomb of Queen Maguncia, of Candaya, and Peter of

Provence rode it when he made off with beautiful Magalona.

Merlin was the name of its maker, and the horse was so constructed that it could be governed by turning a wooden peg in its forehead. The name means "wooden peg." A comprehensive description of these incidents may be found in the fourth and fifth chapters of the third book of "Don Quixote," but the description is not of sufficient interest to be quoted here.

The story of the Cid's horse, to date back to an earlier century, is almost as well known as the story of Rosinante. The Cid's horse died some two and a half years after its master's death, and during the whole of that period none rode it, the order having gone forth that under no circumstances was anybody to mount the animal. At its death its body was buried near the gate of the monastery at Valencia, two trees being planted close to the grave to mark its whereabouts.

According to the popular legend, the horse acquired its name through Rodrigo's having, when told in his youth that he might select a horse, chosen an almost valueless colt. His godfather, annoyed at this display of ignorance, at once nicknamed the lad "the dolt," which nickname Rodrigo presently conferred upon the horse itself. Literally, however, "Cid" is Arabic for "lord."

Among the few traits in the character of Mary Queen of Scots that have not formed subjects for controversy among the many biographers of that ill-starred sovereign, her undoubted fondness for animals stands out prominently.

From first to last I have read many biographies of Mary Queen of Scots, and it is remarkable that no two coincide consistently in their statements, from which we are forced to the conclusion that the majority of such works have been produced by writers who either were bigoted or deeply prejudiced, or else who had some private axe to grind.

With regard to Mary's horses, her two chief favourites would appear to have been Rosabelle—the animal at one time worshipped by a proportion of the body of minor poets!—and Agnes, called after Agnes of Dunbar, a countess in her own right. This palfrey—almost all the horses of the period of Mary Queen of Scots are spoken of as "palfreys"—apparently came as a gift from her brother, Moray, and though it does not appear to have been a steed of exceptional quality she was extraordinarily fond of it. We find it referred to occasionally as Black Agnes.

Then, though all the evidence obtainable tends to convey the impression that Mary Queen of Scots must have been a clever horsewoman, she does not appear to have been very fond of hunting, in consequence of which two at least of her biographers go so far as to hint that her alleged distaste for the chase tended in a measure to increase Elizabeth's hostility towards her.

From what early historians tell us, Mary probably looked far better on a horse than Elizabeth ever did—the slimness alone of Mary's figure by contrast with Elizabeth's may have been in a measure responsible for this—and the knowledge must have vexed Elizabeth, who took particular pride in her riding and was desirous above many other things to be deemed a finished horsewoman. How vast a number of horses must have been owned by the nobles and by other persons of wealth who dwelt scattered over the whole of England may be gathered from the statement of Ralph Holinshed that Queen Elizabeth alone required, when she travelled, some 2400 animals, almost all of which had to be provided by residents in the districts in which she moved.

The majority of these horses were employed to drag the great carts which contained the queen's baggage, yet we are told that "the ancient use of somers and sumpter horses" having been "utterly relinquished, causeth the trains of our princes in their progresses to show far less than those of the kings of other nations."

Naturally it must be borne in mind that the weight of the baggage of persons of rank in the sixteenth century was excessive, especially when it was added to the weight of the clumsy carts that were used for the conveyance of such baggage, so that four, six and even more horses were often enough harnessed to a single cart when it was fully loaded.

Then, too, the roads were for the most part in so bad a state of repair—many of them could not, properly speaking, be called roads at all—that frequent changes of horses were necessary.

———————

In Drayton's well-known "Polyolbion" we have a horse that is very famous in romance. Arundel by name—a name that is said to have been originally a corruption of the French word, *hirondelle*—it was "swifter than the swiftest swallow." This horse belonged to Bevis of Southampton, "the remarkable knight," and apparently it had as many good points as any animal can possess. In the sixteenth century almost every horse of note actually living, or in romance, took its name from one or other of its chief characteristics. Thus in Tasso's "Jerusalem Delivered" we find Raymond's steed, Aquiline, that was bred on the banks of the Tagus, particularly remarkable for what we should to-day call a Roman nose.

Aquiline figures largely in "Jerusalem Delivered," and Raymond, who was Count of Toulouse and commander of some 4000 infantry, and who, in addition, was remarkable for his wisdom and coolness in debate, is shown to have owed a measure of his success to Aquiline's phenomenal sagacity. Indeed Aquiline probably saved him from destruction upon more than one occasion.

We come upon other horses in several portions of "Jerusalem Delivered," especially in connection with the slaying by Raymond of Aladine, the cruel old king. The stirring description of this incident, and of the planting of the Christian standard upon the tower of David by Raymond, is to be found in the twentieth book; but as we know that the Holy Land was being ruled by the Caliph of Egypt at the very time Raymond is supposed to have been attacking King Aladine, it at once becomes obvious that the narrative must have been fictitious.

———————

"The Faerie Queene" is another classic in which we find interesting allusions to horses, mostly the horses of romance.

One of the best known of these animals is Brigadore, called sometimes Brigliadore, which belonged to Sir Guyon, and was remarkable for a black mark in its mouth, in shape like a horseshoe.

Sir Guyon, who impersonated Temperance or Self-Government, was the companion of Prudence, and he alludes several times to Brigadore. His fame, as most scholars will remember, rests in a great measure upon his destruction of the enchantress, Acrasia, in the bower called the Bower of Bliss, which was situated in the Wandering Island.

The name Acrasia means self-indulgence, and this witch was particularly dreaded because of her partiality for transforming her lovers into monstrous shapes and then keeping them captive.

The story of Sir Guyon's stealthy approach while Acrasia lay unsuspectingly in her bower, and of the way in which he succeeded in throwing a net over her, subsequently in binding her firmly in chains of adamant, then in breaking down "her accursed bower" and burning it to ashes, is too well known to need description here, and of course it has no direct bearing upon Brigadore.

So far as we can judge, the horses of Anatolia and Syria must have been well known in Europe by about the middle of the sixteenth century, though one or two writers aver that they did not come over until later.

An artist who died about the year 1603, and whose name was Stradamus, produced, not long before his death, a series of drawings, and a set of these was subsequently issued under the title, "Equile Johannis Ducis Austriaci," which means, "The Stable of Don John of Austria."

It is interesting to note in this connection that practically all the horses and mares imported between the year 1660 and the year 1685 came from Smyrna, though the renowned Darley Arabian and several more came from Aleppo.

This is of particular importance in relation to the records of the horse in England's history, for there can be no doubt that a great part of our thoroughbred racing stock is descended from these very early importations.

That remarkable feats of horsemanship were performed in the reign of Elizabeth is beyond dispute, but unfortunately the particulars obtainable are extremely meagre.

Of Sir Robert Carey's historic ride upon the death of the queen, details worth recording are given. No sooner had the queen breathed her last, we are told, than Sir Robert Carey, notorious sycophant that he was, who for days and nights had been loitering about the queen's bed-chamber and displaying the keenest anxiety as to her condition, set off on horseback to convey to the heir, King James, the news of her death.

"So great was his desire to bring the news to King James before that monarch had heard it from any other source," we read, "that with the lamentations of the dead queen's women still ringing in his ears he left the bedside of his kinswoman and benefactress and started to announce the important tidings to King James, an act quite as indelicate as it was wholly unauthorised."

Sir Robert's indelicacy, or alleged indelicacy, however, is no concern of ours. As a feat of endurance, his ride was truly an extraordinary one, for he actually galloped the whole distance from London to Edinburgh, about 400 miles, in less than sixty hours, though during the journey he had at least one severe fall.

How many horses he rode I have not been able to ascertain, but that he had made in advance full preparations for this journey is more than likely, as it is beyond dispute that he had covered the first 160 miles by nightfall on the day after he started. The exact time at which he set out we are not told.

What made the feat more wonderful still was the condition of nearly all the roads in England during

Elizabeth's reign, with the exception of the Roman roads and a few besides, some north of Doncaster being really little more than tracks.

That Sir Robert Carey was well repaid for his enterprise may be gathered from the statement that King James I. "rewarded him for being the first to bring him the glad news, by granting him signal favours."

———————

From about this period onward the horse may be said to have entered upon the third phase of its career in the history of all nations, but more especially in the history of our own nation. For, as we have seen, from very early times down to the period of the Norman Conquest the nations that had not horses had almost without exception been forced to take a secondary place in the world's progress.

From the period of the Norman Conquest down to the beginning of the accession of the House of Stuart—indeed, as we shall see presently, almost down to the period of the Commonwealth—the improvement and development of the horse as an "arm" in warfare had gone practically hand in hand with the improvement in the training of men to fight in battle. And from then onward, that is to say from the beginning of the period of the Stuarts and the Commonwealth, down to the present day, the horse has been connected with history in the capacity of charger or war horse, hunter or pleasure horse, and thoroughbred or race horse.

Let me state at once, then, that it is not my intention to describe at length, or even to mention by name, all the more or less famous, horses that have been owned by the more prominent or distinguished men at any time within the last three hundred years, for such a collection of names, or of descriptions, would not be likely to prove of interest to the modern reader. In addition comparatively few of the records concerning these animals bear the impress of truth.

As we come to the close of the nineteenth and the opening of the twentieth centuries historical records increase enormously in volume, so that now we find ourselves confronted by a mass of reports, many of which bear directly upon horses that are of no interest whatever, though they may have belonged to famous men whose names are still household words.

Thus in a single history of Napoleon I. we find two pages of descriptive matter to do with a horse of his called Wagram; two pages about Cyrus, another of his horses; a page about his horse named Emir; half-a-page about his Coco; three pages about Gongalve; two about Coquet; three about Tausis, and so on all the way through, while everything that is said about them could quite easily be condensed into three or four short sentences.

Indeed the biographers of the majority of our great military leaders have deemed it necessary to write long and verbose descriptions of the animals that were owned by these historical celebrities, apparently for no other reason than that they did belong to celebrities.

When all is said, it is difficult to imagine how or whence they can have obtained such circumstantial information. Granting, however, the truth of all the statements—and one cannot say definitely that any one of them is not true in every detail—was it worth while to tell us that Piers Gaveston owned a grey, or that Blucher remarked upon some uninteresting occasion that he had a horse that used to jib?

Yet trivial points of this sort are to be found mentioned in plenty of the so-called popular biographies of our great men.

Of more interest it would have been had the biographers succeeded in discovering, and then told us, what sort of bits Napoleon liked to ride his chargers in, and his reason or reasons for preferring them, or whether Blucher ever tried his grey in blinkers. Then the horses described at such weary length might possibly have taught us a lesson or two worth learning.

PART III

FROM THE STUART PERIOD TO THE PRESENT DAY

CHAPTER I

"KING JAMES I.'s love of racing," writes a trustworthy chronicler of the movements at the court of James I. and Charles I. "was due to the importation into England of the first Arab horse ever seen here."

That simple statement records one of the most important incidents that has occurred in the development of the horse in this country, an incident that subsequently proved to be of great moment in connection with the history of Great Britain. For though the assertion has many times been controverted, careful research proves beyond doubt that until the arrival in England of the Markham Arabian — which in after generations was to become so greatly renowned—no Arab of any sort had been brought into this country.

STATUE OF COLLEONI BY VERROCCHIO IN VENICE

The stories that have been told of this, the first of the famous Eastern sires, are numerous, and, as is usual in such cases, the majority of them are apparently untrue.

One of the most widely circulated of the misstatements was to the effect that the price paid by King James to Mr Markham for this particular Arab sire was not less than £500, and in papers and books almost innumerable, in which the Markham Arabian is mentioned, this false statement is repeated.

That it is false beyond dispute is proved by the actual entry of the purchase that may be seen to this day in the Exchequer or Receipt Order Books in the Public Record

Office. The entry runs as follows:—

"Item the 20th of December, 1616, paid to Master Markham for the Arabian Horse for His Majesty's own use, £154, 0. 0."

It is almost inconceivable that anyone can seriously have believed that £500, or any sum approaching it, could have been paid for this sire, for at that period no sum approaching £500 ever was paid for any horse, the purchasing value of money being until after the reign of James I. so much in excess of its purchasing value some two centuries later.

That several thoroughbred Eastern sires were bought by James is well known, among the last to which reference is made by the historians being the famous Villiers Arabs, which the king does not appear to have acquired until towards the end of his reign.

Yet in spite of all that has been said and written about John Markham's stallion, the horse was not, according to that excellent judge of horses, the Duke of Newcastle, the class of animal that any man would have chosen to breed from for looks, for, in the duke's own words, "He [the Markham Arabian] was a bay, but a little horse, and no rarity for shape; for I have seen many English horses far finer.... Mr Markham sold him to the King for five hundred pounds (*sic*), and being trained up for a course, when he came to run, every horse beat him."

I believe I am right in saying that the identity of John Markham has never been positively traced, also that the consensus of opinion inclines to the belief that he was the father of the famous author, Gervase Markham, who for many years held the post of keeper of Clipston Shraggs Walk, in Sherwood Forest.

Among the works of Gervase Markham is a volume entitled "Cavalarice, or the English Horseman," in which many grotesque and unintentionally humorous passages are to be found.

Each of the eight books which together go to make up this work is dedicated to some distinguished personage, of whom James I. is one, and Henry, Prince of Wales, another.

To James I. we are probably indebted for the existence of the town of Newmarket, for it is certain that he not only inaugurated the construction of the village, but in addition brought his influence to bear upon its development, and that he greatly helped to stimulate the interest which the people of Newmarket and the neighbourhood already took in the breeding and training of running horses. It may be partly for this reason that Newmarket is still so often spoken of as "the royal village."

Notwithstanding the disappointment the Markham Arabian must have afforded James I., we read that the king offered a silver bell of considerable value to be run for at Newmarket, that the entries for the race were numerous, and that "the event gave rise to much speculation, wagering and public interest."

It was, indeed, in this connection that Ben Jonson wrote so caustically, or rather satirically, in his famous "Alchemist," and alluded incidentally to "the rules to cheat at horse races."

Elsewhere Jonson describes, and mentions by name, some of the race horses that probably were well known on the Turf at about that period.

Seeing how keen the interest was that James I. took almost from boyhood in all that related to the Turf, and to the breeding of race horses, we can hardly be surprised to hear that during his reign the general interest in the breeding of "great horses," which had been so marked a feature of Henry VIII.'s reign, also of Elizabeth's reign, at one time threatened to die out.

Robert Reyce speaks of this in his "Breviary of Suffolk," a book which he dedicated to Sir Robert Crane, of Chiltern, and elsewhere allusions are to be found to the decay of interest in the breeding of "great horses."

Indeed James appears to have admitted quite openly that the bare sight of the animals bored him "owing to the clumsy appearance they presented," a view that is shared to-day by several of the more prominent of our owners of race horses.

Under the circumstances it is amusing to find the king himself inditing a ponderous treatise "for the instruction and edification of his son," Henry, Prince of Wales, a treatise suitably enough entitled "Religio Regis: or the Faith and Duty of a Prince."

Apparently he wrote the greater part of this work at Newmarket, for in it he alludes more than once to the races which were being held there at the time, races at which he had been present on the day he wrote.

That he deemed horsemanship to be a form of exercise of inestimable value becomes obvious as we read "Religio Regis"; but then in the reign of almost every monarch from about the beginning of the Stuart period down to the time of the four Georges great stress is laid by the various sovereigns upon the advisability that the sons of the nobles and of the aristocracy should become proficient horsemen.

The author of "The Court of King James" also is emphatic in his advice to courtiers "to be very forwardly inclined to bring up horses," adding that such horses should be bred from the best strains only, and that no matter how great the sum expended in order to secure good strains, the money could not be looked upon as wasted.

Of the royal studs in the reign of James I., the most important probably were those at Newmarket, at Eltham, at Tutbury, Malmesbury and Cole Park, and among the manuscripts in the British Museum there may be seen to-day an interesting list of the "necessaries" which appertained to the royal stables, all classified under separate headings—geldings, cart horses, coursers, hunters, battle horses, and so on.

Remarks upon the part played by the horse in history at about this time are to be found also in Lodge's "Illustrations of British History," where, in the third volume, we read that on 6th April 1605 there arrived at Greenwich Palace "a dozen gallant mares, all with foal, four horses, and eleven stallions, all coursers of Naples."

These the archduke begged King James to accept as a small mark of the esteem in which the king was held by himself and his country-men.

In the historical records of almost the whole of James I.'s reign we find reference made repeatedly to race horses, also to the sport of hunting. An important fixture, as we should call it to-day, apparently was the Chester Meeting. It took place on St George's Day, and the chief race was known as "The St George's Cup." The riders carried ten stone, and the entrance stake was half-a-crown.

A quaint rule in connection with this race was that the winning owner had to contribute to a fund for the benefit of the prisoners confined in the North Gate jail "the sum of six shillings and eightpence or three shillings and fourpence, on certain conditions."

In addition to the cup, silver bells were run for at this meeting, and it is interesting to learn that before removing their prizes the cup winner and the bell winners were compelled to deposit "adequate security"—presumably with the race committee—for these trophies. For all the principal trophies had to be run for again at the following meeting, and we are told quite seriously that it was feared that if the temporary owners were allowed to remove these prizes without leaving any security they might have been disposed to make away with them before the date of the next meeting!

At the Chester Meeting, and therefore presumably elsewhere, the sheriff acted as starter, "and if any rider committed foul play during the race he was disqualified in case he won."

About the year 1624, however, certain changes were made in the rules of racing, and from that time onward some of the races were run five times round the course instead of only three times, also the winner of a cup became entitled to retain it as his property "upon the first occasion of gaining it."

Professional jockeys in the reign of James I. held, in a sense, quite a good position. The king associated with them frequently, especially at Newmarket. Indeed, he openly admitted that he preferred the company of sportsmen to that of politicians, and that the surroundings of the racecourse and the pleasures of the chase attracted him far more than did the business of the state.

His enemies, as we know, took advantage of these carelessly uttered assertions when later they set to work to encompass his downfall, and during the closing years of his reign he was made to suffer unjustly for many of the minor follies of his youth.

It was wholly characteristic of James that he should upon one occasion—he was staying at Croydon at the time in order to attend the race meeting that was held there in Easter week—have in a sudden access of emotional enthusiasm created his friend, Philip Herbert, a knight, a baron and a viscount in the course of a few minutes.

This he is said to have done in order to mark his appreciation of Herbert's self-control when, after being struck in the face by a Scotsman named Ramsey, Herbert refrained from hitting back.

Though the king and all his courtiers and many strangers were present upon the occasion, Herbert did not betray the least sign of annoyance, though the blow was a severe one.

It should be borne in mind that during James's reign the Scots had, as a nation, come to be almost execrated, so that the affront was all the greater.

The king is said to have expressed it as his opinion that under the circumstances Philip Herbert's self-restraint came near to being heroic!

As James's fondness for racing increased, so did the great majority of his nobles, his barons and his courtiers profess to grow fonder of the sport, while many soon took to gambling with great recklessness.

This the king apparently encouraged them to do, for we learn that he was "wont to laugh heartily when told that some of his sycophants had lost exceptionally large sums of money," or, as was frequently the case, that one or other of them had been compelled to part with a portion of his estates in order to meet debts of honour. The women of the court also aped the king at this time, as indeed they appear to have done in almost every age. Yet their losses were small by comparison with the sums lost on the Turf by their daughters and granddaughters in the reign of Charles II., half-a-century or so later.

Two years after James I. had ascended the throne there set in one of the coldest winters this country has ever known, with the result that a long stretch of the River Ouse became frozen over and so afforded the king an opportunity, of which he was quick to avail himself, of organising a race-meeting on the ice.

Drake tells us that the course extended "from the tower at the end of Marygate, under the great arch of the bridge, to the crane at Skeldergate Postern."

But even so early as this in the reign of King James the opponents of horse racing began to raise indignant protests against "the folly and wickedness of betting on running horses," protests to which but scant attention was paid.

Not until some years later did the extremely zealous clergyman named Hinde set seriously to work to denounce the practice of gambling in any and every form, and he appears then to have spoken and written so forcibly that many persons of intelligence and education—I quote from a trustworthy source—gathered round and strove to encourage him to the best of their ability.

Racing in particular he waged war against, declaring it to be "an exercise of profaneness diligently followed by many of our gentlemen and by many of inferior rank also." Great injury, he maintained, was done by men of rank and others "who of their weekly and almost daily meetings, and matches on their bowling greens, or their lavish betting of great wagers in such sorry trifles, and of their stout and strong abbeting of so sillie vanaties amongst hundreds, sometimes thousands, of rude and vile persons to whom they should give better, and not so bad example and encouragement, as to be idle in neglecting their callings; wasteful in gaming, and spending their means; wicked in cursing and swearing, and dangerously profane in their brawling and quarrelling."

These observations, and many more to the same effect, are to be found in the "Biography of Bruen"; yet in the long run the diatribes made but little difference, for the passion for gambling had taken a firm hold of the people of almost all classes, and while it lasted it flourished exceedingly.

We do not hear of many famous horses during the reign of James I., save the sires which the king himself imported; yet it is certain that the popularity of the horse increased during the first two decades of the seventeenth century, quite apart from the popularity that betting upon horse races continued to acquire.

As a natural result, perhaps, greater attention soon came to be paid to the management and care of horses, to feeding and exercising them, so that probably the owners of the thoroughbreds of those days had begun to realise, as they do not appear to have done before, that a horse's working years may be considerably prolonged if he be fed carefully and exercised regularly.

Indeed the crass ignorance that until about this time had prevailed with regard to the treatment of sick horses comes near to being ludicrous. Superstition, as we know, was rampant in connection with the curing of suffering humanity, and various forms of superstition extended in a great measure to the treatment of animals that were out of health.

Thus we read of horses supposed to be possessed by evil spirits, when what they probably were suffering from was an attack of simple staggers; of witches being consulted when a horse went lame, and paid liberally for their grotesque advice, and so on to the end.

That horses so often went lame at about this period was due probably to the ignorance of many of the farriers of the very rudiments of practical farriery.

In Ireland, possibly also in parts of England, a horse with what is called to-day a "wall" eye was looked upon as a harbinger of evil, and deemed likely to bring bad luck, especially upon the family and relatives of the man who owned it; while any man so "ill-advised" as to breed a fearsome creature of this kind often was afterwards glanced at askance by persons who before he had numbered amongst his friends.

Then there existed also a superstitious belief in connection with a horse with a white hoof, but what this particular superstition was I have not been able to discover. Apparently the owner of a horse so marked was glad enough to get rid of it for a sum much below its true worth, and generally he deemed himself fortunate if able to sell such a horse at all.

An instance is on record of a weakly foal being left out all night in a snowstorm as a superstitious test. We are told that it died of exposure, and that its owner at once thanked God for His mercy in having taken from him a creature born with an evil spirit, the inference being that but for the alleged evil spirit the little foal would have been able to withstand the rigour of the blizzard and the intense cold.

Stolen horses in particular were believed to possess a supernatural power that would enable them to find their way home to their rightful masters if they succeeded in escaping from the thief. But plenty of horses, as we know, are to-day able to find their way home from a long way off, horses that have not necessarily been stolen.

In justice let it be said that James laughed to scorn the majority of these superstitious beliefs. This is strange, for in some respects he must have been almost as superstitious as many of his courtiers—and for that matter as the great bulk of his subjects.

Partial to tall horses, he expressed a wish that his nobles should not ride cobs, deeming such animals to be out of keeping with the majesty of the court.

It was probably for this reason that he strove to encourage his subjects to ride tall horses.

Then, though several historians appear to take it for granted that the Turkish horse was unknown in England until the arrival of the famous Byerley Turk in 1689, we may rest assured that Turkish horses were here in James's time, and probable before his time. Blunderville is only one of the early writers who say so in so many words. Incidentally he mentions that fully a century before the Byerley Turk was brought over he himself had seen "horses come from Turkey, as well into Italie as thither into England, indifferentlie faire to the eie, tho' not verie great nor stronglie made, yet very light and swift in their running, and of great courage."

Also we read that about the year 1617 "half-a-dozen Barbry horses" were brought to England by Sir Thomas Edmonds and stabled at Newmarket in the royal paddocks.

A quaint description is to be found in the works of several of the writers in James I.'s reign of an accident that befell the king in December of the year 1621 as he was riding after dinner, an accident that in spite of its undeniable grotesqueness might well have proved disastrous.

The king, it seems, had "gone abroad early in the day, and to Theobald's to dinner." He appears to have enjoyed his dinner at Theobald's greatly, and to have decided quite suddenly, as soon as the meal was over, that he would like "to ride on horseback abroad."

The accident that presently was to occur is attributed by different writers to different causes, the most charitable of the reports being to the effect that the king's horse stumbled and threw his royal master on to the frozen surface of the New River "with so much violence that the ice brake and he fell in so that nothing but his boots were seen."

Sir Richard Young, who chanced to be riding just behind him, instantly sprang off his horse and succeeded with the help of a friend, though only with great difficulty, in dragging the dripping monarch "out of the hole and his undignified predicament."

According to another chronicler, "there came much water out of his mouth and body," yet "His Majesty rid back to Theobald's, went into a warme bed, and, as we heere, is well, which God continue."

That the king had a sense of humour is made manifest by the statement that upon his recovery he laughed heartily at the recollection of the incident, while we are further told that his gratitude to Sir Richard Young, his rescuer, "did not stop short at the hearty grasp of the hand he gave him."

Mention has already been made of James's strange literary work, "Religio Regis: or the Faith and Duty of a Prince." This is said to have been written during the King's temporary residence at Newmarket "for the betterment of his health" (*sic*).

It was produced primarily for "the instruction and edification" of his son, Henry, at that time Prince of Wales, but it came to be read widely by his nobles and all about the court.

In this remarkable treatise we are told that "the honourablest and most commendable Games that a king can use are on Horseback, for it becomes a Prince above all Men to be a good Horseman. And use such Games on Horseback as may teach you to handle your Arms thereon, such as Tilt, Ring, and low-riding for handling your sword....

"As for hunting, the most honourable and noblest Sport thereof is with running Hounds; for it is a thievish sport of hunting to shoot with Guns and Bows....

"However, in using either of these Sports observe such Moderation that you slip not therewith Hours appointed for your Affairs, which you ought ever precisely to keep; remembering that these Pastimes are but ordain'd for you to enable you for your Office, to which you are call'd by your Birth."

Before the close of James's reign the Turf bore every sign of having been granted a fresh lease of life. Private riding matches among men of rank and wealth had become popular again, and though some of these were "'cross-country matches," plenty were ridden on the flat, upon which occasions vast sums of money were run for almost always.

Of these races one that seems to have attracted much attention was run in the year 1622, for a cup valued at twelve pounds, when the crowd that assembled was one of the biggest at that time on record.

The wagers that were made were mostly in large sums, and we are told that, to the surprise of the majority of the betting men "and their subsequent discomfiture," the race, in which there were six "tryers," was won by an outsider, the property of a popular sportsman, Sir George Bowes.

The judge in this race was a Mr Humphrey Wyvell, and so greatly annoyed did the crowd become at the defeat of the favourite that they made a desperate attempt to attack the judge, with the intention of injuring him seriously, an attempt that fortunately was frustrated.

We are not told if the king was present upon this occasion, but the principal racing men of the period undoubtedly were there. The king himself attended a meeting at Lincoln in the spring of 1617, where he lost very heavily.

Towards the end of this reign strong opposition to the increasing popularity of racing began to manifest itself among what we should to-day call the middle class, owing, so it was said, to the sport being vigorously denounced from pulpit and platform as a growing national evil, "one likely to imperil the whole country's prosperity."

For some time the king strove to smother these denunciations, and he even partially succeeded in the attempt.

Yet in the end the people must have triumphed, for we read that James was still on the throne when some of the more popular of the flat-race meetings were tacitly allowed to be abandoned, while in 1620 the meeting which usually had been held at Thetford was directly suppressed by an order of the Privy Council.

Among the most important of the private riding matches, as they were then called, that took place in James's reign was the one arranged at Newmarket between Lord Haddington and Lord Sheffield.

Run at Huntingdon towards the end of the year 1607, the

race was extremely exciting from start to finish. Both men appear to have been good riders, and the stake run for is said to have amounted to a considerable sum.

Yet the various accounts of the match give versions which differ widely as to what happened, and while one writer declares that Lord Haddington won with difficulty, another contradicts him by maintaining that the stake was awarded to Lord Sheffield.

With regard to the pictures that are said to have been drawn from life in those days, if they are true to life it becomes obvious that some three centuries ago it was not customary for race riders, or "tryers," to stand in their stirrups while riding races, as they do to-day and most certainly did in the last century and the century before it. This is strange, for some of the earliest of our writers who touch incidentally upon the subject of race riding are rather emphatic in declaring that the jockey should get rid of all "dead" weight, and of course it is chiefly by standing in the stirrups that "dead" weight can be neutralised.

James I. would seem to have paid more attention to the theory of training horses he intended to run than any of his predecessors did, though this is not great praise, so ignorant of the fundamental principles of scientific training were the horse owners of about that period.

Upon slight provocation horses were freely bled, just as human beings were bled or "leeched" less than a hundred years ago. Indeed we read of one horse that was bled while in the hunting field, owing to its having proved too restive for its owner to ride with comfort (!); while another was driven into a leech pond in order that the leeches might suck off "the goodlie warts" with which its belly and thighs were studded.

So far as I have been able to ascertain, about a century and a half ago the leech cure was deemed quite the best for warts. Yet perhaps we are wrong to think or to speak contemptuously of the ignorance of our forefathers. Who can say that in years to come our descendants may not speak as contemptuously of us—their ancestors—because we fired horses, and because we drenched them with physic for various ailments?

Indeed there are already veterinary surgeons who aver that to fire a horse under any circumstances is to commit a grave blunder, and that firing as a general practice ought emphatically to be abandoned.

CHAPTER II

THE early history of Newmarket is more or less wrapped in mystery, or rather in confusion; in other words, the writers who have dealt with "the inauguration of Newmarket racing," as one of them terms it, in many instances contradict one another so flatly that the truth can be arrived at only by conjecture or by inference.

Apparently the destruction of the Spanish Armada in 1588 was the ill wind that indirectly benefited Newmarket so far as its horses were concerned, for there is no doubt that many of the horses rescued from drowning when the great vessels of the Armada were wrecked were sent direct to Newmarket, "where great surprise was expressed by all who beheld them at their exceeding swiftness."

From this one would naturally conclude that interesting races were run on Newmarket Heath towards the close of the sixteenth century; yet elsewhere we read that the first races of importance run at Newmarket took place in 1640, and that the round course was not made until about the year 1666, while a third historian goes so far as to declare that a gold cup run for at the Newmarket Spring Meeting of

1634 affords *per se* the earliest irrefutable record of such an occurrence, based on contemporary data.

Yet from statements set down in an earlier chapter we have already seen that horse racing of a sort must have taken place at Newmarket quite a long time before this. In point of fact, in almost every historical record of Newmarket that I have come upon I have found either direct or indirect allusion to the renown of the neighbourhood of Newmarket for the horses that were bred or trained there.

The horses brought ashore from the Spanish vessels probably were among the best that Spain at that time possessed, and several attempts were made by the Spanish to recover some of them. It is known that towards the close of the sixteenth century the Spanish were making determined efforts to breed faster horses than they had previously bred, yet it is surprising that the horses they had brought with them upon their famous expedition should have been so swift, for they must have been animals of far heavier type than the animals they would in a general way breed for racing.

The Spaniards of three centuries ago, we must of course remember, were renowned for their horsemanship far more highly than their descendants of to-day are.

In the reign of Charles I. horse races were run in Hyde Park, a track having been laid down there with great care. This meeting was immensely popular, and "the inhabitants of London and those parts near London assembled in their thousands to watch the running horses," and in most instances to squander large sums.

"The Park first became under Charles I. the fashionable society rendezvous," Mrs Alec Tweedie tells us in her interesting volume, "Hyde Park: Its History and Romance."

"Its greatest attraction, maybe, was the racing in the Ring. The occasions when organised meetings took place were special scenes of gaiety, and were evidently thought important events, as even among the State Papers there is preserved the agreement for a race that took place there."

In later years an attempt was made to revive the Hyde Park race meeting, but the attempt was vigorously opposed by the mass of the residents in the neighbourhood, and by many others as well.

A report of a race in Hyde Park appears in a copy of *The London Post*, but is undated. As *The London Post* ceased to exist after the year 1640, this race was run probably a year or two before that date. The report is said to be the first detailed account of a horse race ever published in a newspaper.

"I made a present to the King," Sully writes, "of six beautiful horses richly caparisoned, and the Sieur of St Antoine as their keeper." The Sieur of St Antoine, who after being equerry to Prince Henry became equerry to Charles I., is represented in the famous Vandyck picture of King Charles in armour, in the picture now in the National Gallery.

VAN DYCK'S FAMOUS PICTURE, NOW IN THE NATIONAL GALLERY,
OF CHARLES I ON HORSEBACK

It was about the year 1641 that the Duke of Buckingham greatly helped to improve the breed of horses by importing the famous Helmsley Turk and the almost equally famous Morocco Barb. It is curious to read that the importation of

211

these horses was at first looked upon with grave suspicion by a great body of the principal horse breeders in this country, and by others interested in the horse and its development.

To what the antagonism was owing one can hardly say for certain. One report has it that some among the duke's personal enemies—he had many enemies—were determined to do all in their power to injure him by wrecking any scheme in which he presumably was interested. The sums he paid for these horses were considerable, but the excellent effect the good blood had upon the breed fully repaid him for the incidental outlay, also for the great trouble to which he had been put to secure such excellent stallions.

Shortly before this some English officers serving in the Dutch army had introduced horse racing into Holland, and the popularity of the new sport began to spread there quickly. Soon a number of race meetings came to be organised, and in a short time Dutch emissaries were sent over to England for the express purpose of purchasing blood stock here.

Being comparatively ignorant of horses—ignorant, that is to say, of the requirements essential in a racing stallion—these emissaries were at first cheated in the most barefaced manner by some of the very men who only a short time before had been their guests in Holland!

Later, however, they succeeded in importing some very valuable blood stock, and in several respects the race meetings they presently organised were better arranged than many of the English meetings of that period.

In 1637 we find the Duke of Newcastle appointed Governor to Prince Charles—later to become King Charles II.—with special injunctions to teach him to ride well.

The duke's volume on equitation, published at Antwerp in 1658, contains particulars of the prince's progress in the art of horsemanship, from which we may gather that Prince Charlie was an exceptionally apt pupil—"a horseman by nature," he has been termed.

So emphatically was this the case that in comparatively a few years he professed himself able to ride any horse that anyone might choose to bring to him, an assertion in which the duke supported him.

It was not long after this that the duke persuaded his royal pupil to import from Spain a number of exceptionally fine sires, for, as he said, Spanish stallions were quite unsurpassed, and in his opinion no other sort of stallion ought to be admitted into this country.

The duke himself has been described as "an iron horseman," but the exact meaning of the phrase is not quite clear. He had, according to some writers, an "iron" seat on a horse, while according to others he had "iron" hands—the latter a questionable compliment.

Probably an "iron" nerve is what they really meant, for we know that the Duke of Newcastle was both a finished and a fearless horseman, two important qualifications that do not necessarily go together. We are further told that in teaching the prince to ride he never spared him, a statement easily believed when the duke's hard and resolute nature, added to his known determination to succeed at any cost in every task he undertook to accomplish, are borne in mind. Ordered to train the prince into a skilful horseman, he had at once set to work to do it to the best of his ability.

Some say that as a boy Prince Charlie looked, when in the saddle, as if he had been born there, and through life this natural seat upon a horse stood him in good stead.

In addition to being a graceful rider, he had a very strong seat, so that presumably he possessed the precious gift that to-day we call "hands."

An eighteenth-century writer, who appears to have had access to private manuscripts or documents to do with King Charles II.'s private life, avers that the king never, as we should express it, pulled a horse about. Even tempered with his horses, he seldom or never ill-treated them. They appeared to respond instinctively to his every touch, to understand what he meant by the varying inflection in his voice, and to divine, as if by magic, what their master wished them to do. Also he never outrode a horse under any circumstances—never, as we should say, rode a horse off its legs.

He preferred long stirrup leathers to short, but then in his day most men did.

Also it is said of him that he never would look twice at a horse that had bad quarters or indifferent withers.

Altogether it seems clear that, though he had a natural aptitude for horsemanship, he must have been carefully and very thoroughly coached in all the points of a horse, as well as in all that appertained to the management, training and stabling of horses of every kind.

Horses had risen in price during Charles I.'s reign. In the reign of Charles II. they rose higher still.

Thus about the year 1635—that is to say towards the middle of Charles I.'s reign—300 and 400 pistoles was considered a moderate sum to pay for a well-broken young horse.

"And the Marquis of Seralvo told me," writes the Duke of Newcastle, "that a Spanish horse called Il Bravo, and sent to the Arch-Duke Leopold, his master, was held as much as a Mannor of a Thousand Crowns a year, and that he hath known horses at 700, 800, and 1000 pistoles."

Elsewhere we find indisputable evidence that between the beginning of Charles I.'s and the end of Charles II.'s reign sums varying from 400 to 700 pistoles must often have been paid for saddle horses, while for race horses the prices were considerably in excess of these sums.

It is amusing to read that the duke spoke in terms almost of contempt of the Barb, for it shows that in one respect at least he must have been prejudiced in much the same way that some of our modern owners and trainers of thoroughbreds are prejudiced.

Yet he was firmly convinced that many of the horses imported from such countries as Germany, Denmark and Holland were well suited for harness work and for the plough.

In face of this, and in face also of his strong bias in favour of Spanish stallions, it is surprising to hear that he deemed the English horse to be "the best horse in the whole world for all uses whatever, from the cart to the manage," and that he even considered some of them to be "as beautiful horses as can be anywhere, for they are bred out of all the horses of all nations."

Equally enthusiastic upon the subject of the English horse and its merits, and upon its superiority over the horses of other nations, was Marshal de Bassompierre, who has something to say about them in the interesting memoirs of his embassy in England in 1626.

Thus after telling us that during his residence in this

country he received from some of the high officers of state, also from the king himself, a present of fine horses, he goes on to mention incidentally that it was at about this period that English thoroughbreds were introduced into France for the first time.

This is interesting, inasmuch as certain writers of an earlier epoch state definitely that English thoroughbreds were to be seen in parts of France in their day.

Bassompierre, who had been in England in Elizabeth's reign, is likely to have known the true facts. In addition to being "addicted to horses," he was passionately fond of gambling, and the latter hobby is said to have cost him in a single year some £500,000.

A family notorious early in the Stuart era for its devotion to the Turf was the Fenwick family, so much so that several of its members are described as having run "quite out of their fortunes" in their futile attempts to transform two or three small fortunes into one large one. The sensational story of Sir John Fenwick's trial, followed by his execution on Tower Hill in 1697, establishes a sort of landmark in the history of the public executions of the seventeenth century.

During the first half of the same century horse fairs were organised throughout England, and year by year they became events of greater importance, many hundreds of men and women of all ranks travelling from far-distant parts of the country in order to attend them. The scenes of ribaldry by which many of these fairs were followed would not be tolerated now. Among the more important of the fairs were those held at Ripon, Melton, Pankridge and Northampton, but many of the others were almost equally fashionable.

It was in the reign of Charles I. that Sir Edward Harwood presented the famous petition, or memorial, in which he explained in forcible language that "good and stout horses for the defence of the kingdom" would soon be to all intents at a premium owing to the scant attention that was then being paid to the breeding of such animals, adding that he doubted whether, if some 2000 great horses should be wanted at short notice, it would be possible to find so many in a fit condition to do battle.

The French horses of the same stamp, he went on to say, were in almost every way superior to ours, and so emphatic was he upon this last point that he openly declared that if some 2000 of the best of our great horses were to be set face to face in battle with an equal number of the Frenchmen's horses, our troops would to a certainty be routed with heavy loss.

Seeing how earnestly Harwood spoke, the king, as we are told, expressed sorrow and great amazement at what he heard, and at once inquired the reason of the English horses' alleged inferiority.

Then it was that Sir Edward made his point. With considerable bluntness he told the king that the decline of the great horse was due chiefly to the spread of racing and hunting, and to the growth, consequent thereon, in the number of race meetings that were being organised, and in the assemblage of persons who attended them.

For, as he justly pointed out, so long as the attention of the principal body of the nobility and of the wealthy landed proprietors was centred upon the breeding almost wholly of light and swift horses, it was not possible to suppose that time would be found to attend also to the breeding and rearing of the powerful animals that alone were fit to carry men-at-arms.

Upon hearing this, Charles declared, no doubt in all good

faith, that he would take steps to revive the flagging interest in the production of good war horses, but in the end nothing practical was done.

That the king himself took interest in the great horse we are led to infer from the fact that upon the big seal he is shown riding astride one. In Vandyck's portrait of Oliver Cromwell we see Cromwell riding rather a light-coloured great horse, a point worthy of note inasmuch as we know that from about that time onward the term "great" horse was almost always taken to mean a *black* horse of this particular stamp.

OLIVER CROMWELL ON HORSEBACK
After Van Dyck

Oliver Cromwell's world-renowned Ironsides were not, of

course, mounted on great horses. On the contrary, though the Ironsides proved themselves to be by far the most powerful cavalry seen in England down to that time, their strength was due not to their weight, but to their remarkable mobility.

The dismay the Ironsides spread amongst the foe is said to have astonished the cavaliers themselves as much as it surprised the enemy.

For it must be borne in mind that the Ironsides did not wear armour. Instead they were protected merely by light buff coats, so that naturally they were able to ride far lighter and consequently more active, horses.

Probably it was the good work done by Cromwell's cavalry that marked the turning-point in the life of the old *régime* by driving out of the field not only the great horses that until then had been deemed wholly indispensable, but also by sounding the death-knell of armour that for two centuries had been growing steadily heavier and more ponderous.

For many years, however, a body of the English military authorities metaphorically clung doggedly to the clumsy horses to which they had so long been accustomed, and to the clumsy armour as well, declaring—as some of their successors do to-day—that the innovation of a mobile force must soon prove unsatisfactory and ultimately be disbanded.

Instead, exactly the reverse happened.

By slow degrees the armour was discarded, while the great horses, as we are told, were relegated to the coach, the waggon and the plough.

Among those who adhered longest to the theory that

England must inevitably lose her prestige if the great horse were ousted from her army for good and all was the Duke of Newcastle of that period. Laughed at for his pains, and spoken of by the younger generation as a man not able to see ahead of the times, he yet stood firmly by his opinion almost to the last. As the years went on, and the younger generation in their turn grew retrospective and pessimistic, no doubt they too were laughed at by their sons, and thus history continues to repeat itself even to the present day.

———————

At about this period many of the "good" roads in England were in reality little better than broad cart tracks, so that heavy horses were largely in demand. In consequence of this the prices paid for a good team of horses were in many instances out of all proportion to the animals' true worth. By this time, too, public stages were already being started on the highroads, and the competition this gave rise to soon sent up by leaps and bounds the value of great horses well broken to harness.

Of these stages the first was started probably about the year 1670, and its weight when empty must have been enormous, every part being made of solid timber bound with strips of iron. The "speed" at which it travelled—so far as one can gather from the early descriptive records of the progress of the pioneer stage—must have been approximately three or four miles an hour, upon an average, or even less.

An excellent reproduction of the early type of the English great horse is to be seen in Dublin in the famous statue of William III. on horseback. The type of horse shown is probably the exact type that was popular not merely in William III.'s reign, but during the greater part of the century before he ascended the throne.

True, in that statue the king is garbed like an ancient Roman, the reason being—I take the following statement from several Irish jarveys, and disclaim all responsibility for its alleged accuracy—that King William adored a foreigner and tried always to look like one! It was, indeed, a jarvey who remarked as we drove past: "Sure, and it is in hunting kit he should be, and on one of Pat Mecreedy's hundred-guinea leppers." He appeared to be convulsed with mirth at the bare thought that the hero of the Boyne should have been depicted mounted upon a cart horse.

Some even among our historians, however, have averred that this horse is wrongly proportioned. Personally I incline to the belief that the animal is in every detail true to life, and not many years ago the late Viscount Powerscourt declared that he himself had seen used in parts of Holland horses that in every respect resembled this animal of King William's statue.

Is it not likely, therefore, that William III. may have been in the habit of riding a Dutch horse, and that the sculptor copied this horse quite faithfully?

Certainly if the pictures of the period are to be trusted for accuracy, soon after the overthrow of James II. by William of Orange there were horses in plenty of almost exactly this type to be seen in England. Also the harness that was worn by many of the Dutch horses shown in the pictures resembled the harness that was in use among followers of William III., more especially the parts we mean to indicate when we speak of a horse's trappings.

Even the bridles greatly resembled one another in some instances.

Bearing directly upon the story of the horse in history are the descriptions that have been handed down to us of the almost frantic opposition that met the introduction of the stage coach soon after the middle of the seventeenth century.

In some respects these descriptions recall vividly to mind the rabid antagonism some two centuries later to the introduction of the steam engine, not to speak of the objections that are still raised by a proportion of the community to the general adoption of automobilism.

Prior to the introduction of the stage coach into England a four-wheeled carriage with a long, low body had been employed to convey the general public from one part of the country to another, and when the stage coach first arrived many of our wiseacres were quick to prophesy that the death-knell of the nation's greatness had in consequence been sounded!

Perhaps one of the stoutest of the opponents of reform in this respect was a certain Mr Cressett, of Charterhouse, who in the year 1662 openly and in very straightforward language affirmed that the adoption of the stage coach must "entirely ruin the country," and who in that year wrote a vigorous tract, in which he explained entirely to his satisfaction—also, apparently, to the satisfaction of his partisans—that the amount of harm the introduction of road coaching must inevitably cause to the community at large would be enormous.

His remarks, too voluminous to reprint *in extenso*, contain in one place the observation that "by this rapid mode of travelling"—at the period in which he wrote it took approximately three days to get from London to Dover, even in fine weather—"gentlemen will come to London upon the slightest pretext, which but for these abominable coaches they would not do but upon urgent necessity."

Nor would the impending evil, in his opinion, end there, for, lashing himself gradually into a fury, he went on to maintain that "the gentlemen's wives" would come too, and that no sooner would they find themselves in London than they would "get fine clothes, go to plays and treats, and by these means get such a habit of idleness and love for pleasure that they would be uneasy ever after."

Poor Mr Cressett!

Surely he must have been an ancestor, or at the least some early relative, of the notorious Mr Wightman who, just before the first London and Brighton railway was laid down, wrote a book in which he "proved" beyond refutation that no locomotive steam engine could by any possibility be propelled at a speed greater than about half the speed of the fastest of the coaches then on the road!

We smile indulgently at all this now, yet, when all is said, have we changed so very greatly since those dark and peculiar ages—since the epoch that we now refer to so complacently as "the good old times"? (sic).

The narratives of the remarkable experiences of many of the travellers in those early coaches would make up almost enough letterpress to fill a volume. For from the very outset the public stages became the unlawful prey of half the rascals with which a vast tract of the whole of England at that time teemed. Coaches were plundered almost daily, and while sometimes blood was spilt intentionally, often this happened rather by accident.

Charles II., who used his influence to help on the development of the stage coach, appears at times to have become frankly impatient with the ultra-conservatism of the bulk of his nobility and of the aristocracy who strove hard to check the progress of the new form of locomotion.

Whatever Charles's shortcomings may have been—and we know that he had many—he had enough of *nous* to be able to foresee the enormous advantages that would be derived from the general adoption of the public stage.

Consequently he encouraged the importation of stallions and the breeding of animals of the stamp best adapted for coach work.

Himself a finished whip, most likely, he desired that all his nobles should emulate his example by learning to drive well, though driving in those days was a form of amusement comparatively seldom indulged in by the well-to-do, who, as we are told, preferred being driven by postillions.

Before Prince Charles's proclamation, however, the ten years of the Commonwealth's sway had to intervene, during which time the horse's progress in this country suffered a set-back from the effects of which it did not immediately recover.

The beginning of the horse's decline in public favour may be said to have dated from 4th January 1651, on which day a report was drawn up—to be soon afterwards presented to Parliament—demanding that horse races, hunting, hawking matches and football playing be at once suppressed, the plea in favour of this radical reform being that frequently political meetings were convened by enemies of the Commonwealth under the veil of race meetings and similar social gatherings.

CHAPTER III

THOUGH it soon became evident that the Commonwealth was determined to oppose, tooth and nail, any step that might in the least tend to keep alive the interest in horse racing and horse breeding that for many years had grown up so steadily throughout almost the length and breadth of England, not until the 3rd July 1654 did the Government finally decide to introduce "an ordinance to prohibit horse racing." This ordinance was duly passed, and the result may well be imagined.

For without further parley almost every racecourse in England was closed, thousands of men of many different grades being thereby at once thrown out of employment. Owners of valuable thoroughbreds lost immense sums, for, practically without warning, they found the order thrust upon them and so were obliged to sell their racing stock for whatever sum it would fetch in the open market.

HORSES OF THE CAVALIERS. SEVENTEENTH CENTURY

In this connection Cromwell, who himself had for many years owned race horses and been very fond of racing, suffered with the rest, though both he and his adherents are said to have declared that they willingly gave up their horses "for the good of the cause they had at heart."

There can be no doubt that many valuable sires were imported into England about the time that Cromwell was practically in power, and one of them, "a south-eastern horse named White Turk," apparently was brought over by Cromwell's own stud groom.

Several of the early records contain interesting descriptions of the sires that were imported at about this time. Mr William Cavendish, afterwards Duke of Newcastle, writing about the year 1658, tells us that the Turkish horse of the period was a tall animal, "but of unequal shape," and that though "remarkably beautiful, very active, with plenty of bone and excellent wind," it rarely had a good mouth.

"The Barb," he writes elsewhere, "possesses a superb and high action, is an excellent trotter and galloper, and very active when in motion. Although generally not so strong as other breeds, when well chosen I do not know a more noble horse, and I have read strange tales of their courage."

The Barbs came of course from Barbary, the best of them from Morocco, Fez, and the adjacent districts, and some from the interior of Tripoli. Even the first to be imported were said to be better shaped than any horses that had been seen before in this country, and to have, in addition, excellent action by nature.

From what can be ascertained at this date, the pure Arabian steed seldom, if ever, stood higher than fourteen and a half hands, and rarely or never became a roarer. In all probability many even of the finest Arabian horses stood but fourteen hands high, while plenty must have been smaller still—say thirteen two or even thirteen one.

This is worth remembering when we know that nearly every horse that has established a reputation on the English Turf has been of Eastern descent.

Probably the best of the Turkish horses were descended from the horses of Arabia and of Persia, though the former were for the most part taller, and generally "bigger built," besides being world renowned for their remarkable docility.

At last the Commonwealth came to an end, and with the accession of Charles II. to the throne "the whole of England," to quote the sentence of a contemporary chronicler, "seemed to open its lungs and breathe again."

For during the ten years of the great Commonwealth the Turf had to all intents become extinct in England. The racecourses were "overgrown and choked," some had been built upon, others had been converted into what purported

229

to be pleasure grounds—"spaces for the recreation of the multitude."

But apparently the multitude preferred the spaces as they had been in the time of Charles I., for no sooner did it become known that the more important of the race meetings that had been abandoned were about to be revived than "the people rejoiced greatly and gave vent to demonstration."

In a surprisingly short time race horses seemed to spring up out of nowhere, some in such good fettle, comparatively —when it is borne in mind that the race horse was supposed to have become practically extinct during the Commonwealth's *régime*—that, as one historian has it, the severity of the laws that had been passed for the suppression of horse racing, and indirectly of race horses, must clearly have been evaded in several parts of this country.

Thus it comes that soon after the Restoration we read of races being run for silver bells and other prizes at Croydon, at Theobald's, at Chester and many other places that had been important racing centres before the Commonwealth.

"Though race horses were few at the time of Charles II.'s accession," observes one writer, "and none had eaten bread for years" (about the middle of the seventeenth century race horses were trained largely on bread), "and these had languished in neglect, at the Restoration they emerged from their obscurity when the penal disabilities collapsed to which the Turf was subjected by the Puritans.

"The revival of horse racing was almost magical in its effects. Thus we find the Turf rising like a Phœnix from its ashes on the accession of Charles II., to be thoroughly reinstated as our great national pastime during the Merry Monarch's reign.

"To this resuscitation the king extended his powerful patronage and support. His love of the equine race is typified in the soubriquet by which he was popularly known, namely 'Old Rowley,' the name of his favourite hack. It is possible that among all our sovereigns, with the exception, perhaps, of Richard II., King Charles II. alone rode his horses first past the winning post. He was, indeed, a thorough English sportsman who could hold his own against all comers in the chases, on the racecourse and so on."

The above description approximately sums up the Merry Monarch so far as his fondness for horses and horse racing has to do with this history. Every inch a horseman, he appears to have been gifted with a singular aptitude for controlling almost any animal he mounted, and to have developed in a high degree the instinct, or whatever it may be, that to-day we speak of as the power of judging pace in race riding.

Endowed with nerve, also with physical courage in abundance, it is not surprising that the king should have been looked upon by many of his courtiers almost as a demigod when first he ascended the throne, and that the Duke of Newcastle, who had trained him to horsemanship, should openly have expressed himself as immensely proud of his pupil and his pupil's skill.

In the principal race at Chester the horses used to run five times round the Roody. It was upon a horse running in this race that Charles once staked and lost a small fortune. The meetings he most preferred, however, probably were those held periodically at Newmarket, where to this day the famous Rowley Mile recalls to memory the seventeenth-century's cheeriest monarch, a king to whom horse racing in this country still owes so much.

231

It was, indeed, King Charles II. who almost entirely rebuilt the stand at Newmarket after the original one had been damaged beyond repair during the progress of the Civil War. It is said that the old race stand was besieged on at least three separate occasions during that long and bloody conflict.

While a certain historic race meeting at Newmarket was in progress, Philip Rotier, the famous sculptor, availed himself of an unexpected opportunity—an opportunity for which he had long waited—to make a sketch of the beautiful Miss Stuart, who was destined to become in the year 1667 the third wife of the third Duke of Richmond.

Miss Stuart's name was at that time in everybody's mouth, the exquisite loveliness of her face being equalled, so it was said, only by the moulding of her figure and the irresistible fascination of her voice and manner. It was this unfinished portrait by Philip Rotier that was subsequently to develop into the figure that to-day we see upon every copper coin—the figure of Britannia with her trident.

"So exact was the likeness," says Felton, in his notes on Waller, "that no one who had ever seen her Grace could mistake who had sat for Britannia."

How rapidly the Turf must have sprung into life once more upon Charles II.'s accession to the throne of England may be gathered from the statement that within six years after the date of his coronation, "the glory of Newmarket had again eclipsed itself." Yet apparently the country's prosperity did not directly benefit. The nobles and the wealthy classes seemed determined at any and every cost to warm both hands at the fire of life in the best and worst meaning of that hackneyed phrase. In Pope's "Imitation of Horace," the statement is made quite bluntly:—

"In days of ease, when now the weary sword
Was sheathed, and luxury with Charles restored,
In every taste of foreign courts improved,
All, by the King's example, lived and loved.
Then peers grew proud in horsemanship t'excell—
Newmarket's glory rose, as Britain's fell."

Wherever in the early histories and records mention is made of Charles's horsemanship, we find also some allusion to William Cavendish, afterwards to become Duke of Newcastle, and credit for Charles's skill is attributed in a great measure to him.

Further we learn that at the age of ten "His Majesty's capacity was such that he would ride leaping horses, and such as would overthrow others, and manage them with the greatest skill and dexterity, to the admiration of all who beheld him."

Indeed in this one respect he must at about that period of his life have resembled the great Alexander, for his determination and self-confidence when he was mounted on horseback were alike amazing. Upon more than one occasion he expressed himself ready to ride for a wager any horse that might be brought to him, and, if need be, to ride it bareback.

In his after life, as we know, this strength of will of his grew gradually into senseless obstinacy, yet he never lost his nerve for riding over a country, a fact the more remarkable when we reflect upon the sort of life he came to lead as he grew older.

The descriptions we have of the race horses he bred are somewhat contradictory and must therefore be received with caution. That he imported many fine mares from Barbary is certain, also it is certain that at regular intervals he sent abroad competent judges with instructions that they should secure for him, regardless of cost, the best animals obtainable.

From among the best of these were selected the stud that came afterwards to be known as the Royal Mares, a designation they bear in the stud-book to this day. The dam of the famous Dodsworth—one of the earliest of all our thoroughbreds—was included in the royal stud, and its pedigree has been authenticated beyond dispute.

Emphatically Charles II. did more to encourage horse racing than any other monarch after Henry VIII. had done, and by comparison he did much more than Henry VIII. by any possibility could have done, the very best racing in Henry's reign being quite inferior to the sport shown in the reign of the Merry Monarch.

And by every means that lay in his power the Duke of Newcastle abetted Charles. The duke himself, soon after the Restoration, sank a considerable sum in the purchase of fresh racing stock to add to his stud, already a large one. And thus the foundation of the thoroughbred stud of modern times may be said to date practically from about the latter part of the seventeenth century.

Thomas Shadwell, the famous playwright, who, born in 1642, lived for half-a-century, alludes in several of his dramatic works to "the great wave of passionate devotion to vices of various kinds" that seemed to roll gradually over the whole of England during the reign of Charles II., while special reference is made to the all-absorbing interest taken in the Turf while the Merry Monarch was on the throne.

Speaking of Newmarket in particular, "there a man is never idle," he makes one of his characters cynically observe, "for we make visits to horses, and talk with grooms, riders and cock-keepers, and saunter in the Heath all the forenoon.

"Then we dine, and never talk a word but of dogs, cocks and horses.

"Then we saunter into the Heath again, then to a cock-match, then to a play in a barn, then to supper, and never speak a word but of dogs, cocks and horses again.

"Then to the Groom Porters, where you may play all night. Oh, 'tis a heavenly life! We are never, never tired!"

Seeing what keen and thorough sportsmen the Irish are, as a body, one is rather surprised to learn that until towards the close of the seventeenth century horse racing was almost unknown in Ireland. No sooner had it been introduced, however, than it began to develop with great rapidity, so that within a few years it spread into many parts of the island and we hear of race meeting after race meeting being organised.

For horse racing seemed to suit the temperament of the Irish people as no other form of sport had done. From the first the Irish must have devoted much time and attention to race horse breeding, and though their facilities for obtaining the services of the best stallions were fewer than the facilities afforded to the English breeders, they yet succeeded in rearing a number of useful animals, while plenty of their race meetings soon compared favourably with some of the best meetings that were held in England at about the same period.

But few particulars are extant of the races in which King Charles himself rode, though several of the earlier writers inform us that he "carried all before him." In a despatch from Sir Robert Carr, dated the 24th day of March 1675, we read that "Yesterday his majestie rode himself three heats and a course and won the Plate, all fower were hard and nere run, and I doe assure you the King wonn by good Horseman Ship."

Descriptions are to be found elsewhere of a fox hunt in which the king took part. It took place some twenty miles from Newmarket. That was in 1680, and apparently no fox hunt in King Charles's reign had before been described in writing.

Yet the king, though partial to hunting, was undoubtedly much fonder of racing. It was in this year—the year 1680—that he entertained at Newmarket the vice-chancellor and the dons of the University of Cambridge, and, as well, all the jockeys who had ridden at the meeting.

Whether vice-chancellor, dons and jockeys were all entertained by the king at the same time is not stated, though we are led to infer that they must have been. Charles, as students of history know, was cosmopolitan to the backbone, and not ashamed of the fact. Ever a practical joker, he is known to have taken delight that was almost boyish in bringing together an assemblage of persons whose sentiments, views and tastes he knew to be in every way dissimilar.

The companionship of jockeys appealed to him at all times, and the year after he had entertained those at Newmarket we find him at supper with the Duke of Albemarle, "and all the jockeys with them." During the progress of this meal Sir Robert Carr and the king arranged several matches in which their respective horses were to be ridden by the jockey each should nominate. That Sir Robert came badly out of the affair may be gathered from the statement that in a single day he lost between £5000 and £6000 "and became greatly enraged"—a breach of etiquette that the king did not forget, and that he never forgave.

A despatch from Lord Conway, dated the 5th April 1682, contains a descriptive account of a false start that took place in one of the races at Newmarket owing apparently to a curious blunder on the part of the starter.

"Here hapned yesterday," Lord Conway writes, "a dispute upon the greatest point of Criticall learning that was ever known at New-Market, A Match between a Horse of Sir Rob: Car's, and a Gelding of Sir Rob: Geeres, for a mile and a halfe only, had engaged all the Court in many thousand pounds, much depending in so short a course to haue them start fairly.

"Mr Griffin was appointed to start them. When he saw them equall he sayd Goe, and presently he cryed out Stay. One went off, and run through the Course and claims his money, the other never stird at all.

"Now possibly you may say that this was not a fayre starting, but the critics say after the word Goe was out of his mouth his commission was determined, and it was illegall for him to say Stay. I suppose there will be Volumes written upon this Subject; 'tis all refered to his Majesty's Judgment, who hath not yet determined it."

Another staunch supporter of horse racing in Charles II.'s reign was the ill-starred Duke of Monmouth, whose career on the English Turf ended abruptly when in 1682 he was practically sent abroad as an exile.

Early in the following year, however, the idea occurred to Louis XIV. that as horse racing had become so popular in England he would like to make it the national pastime of France also. In order to foster public interest in the turf, therefore, he began by offering a plate valued at 1000 pistoles to be run for at Echere, near St Germain.

The event attracted, as he had expected it would, much

attention, not only throughout France, but in several other European countries as well, so that in the end some of the finest horses to be found anywhere in Europe were entered for the race.

All went well until a short time before the date of the race, when a rumour spread mysteriously that a gelding owned by the Hon. Thomas Wharton had been privately backed very heavily by a number of wealthy Englishmen.

At first the report was generally disbelieved. Then suddenly it became known that the famous Duke of Monmouth was to ride the "dark" horse in the big race, and at once the owners of the foreign favourites became seriously alarmed.

That they had good ground for their alarm was soon proved by the duke's steering the English horse to victory, apparently with great ease.

Immediately, so we are told, Louis XIV. cried out in an access of enthusiasm that he must obtain possession of Wharton's horse at any cost. Upon Wharton's informing him that the horse was not for sale, Louis immediately offered to pay "the animal's weight in gold." Thereupon Wharton relented—though not in the way that Louis had expected him to:

"I will not sell the horse," he said, "no, not even for its weight in gold. If, however, your Majesty will do me the honour to accept it as a gift...."

But so generous a proposal Louis flatly declined to entertain, and eventually the horse did not change hands at all. For some weeks afterwards the principal topic of conversation throughout France and part of England was the great race. Indeed it is probable that this single race and the talk that followed it served to stimulate in France a zest for the sport that became far keener than even Louis XIV. had deemed would ever be possible.

THE DUKE OF SCHONBERG ON A TYPICAL CHARGER OF THE

239

Among the more prominent of the race horse's progenitors in the seventeenth century were the Small Bay Arabian, imported by James I.; Burton's Barb Mare; the Helmsley or Buckingham Turk, owned by the Duke of Buckingham; and of course Charles II.'s Dodsworth, a well-shaped, natural Barb, though foaled in England about the year 1670.

Mention has already been made of the Royal Mares, the majority of which were brought over from Tangiers about the year 1669. Towards the beginning of Charles II.'s reign the annual charge for the horses of the king and queen and those of the officers of the royal household was fixed at £16,640—a sum subsequently denounced by the king's enemies as "extravagant beyond belief."

That it was a considerable charge to make all must admit, yet it was not necessarily extravagant beyond measure. For in an age when outward ostentation imparted to the court a sort of cachet, an enormous stud of horses, and those the best obtainable, and in addition innumerable costly trappings, were in a sense necessities—the guarantee and stock-in-trade, so to speak, of a court anxious to gain the world's applause and approval, and indirectly the support of other powerful European nations should war break out, as in King Charles's reign it might well have done at almost any time.

Indeed had Charles's court been indifferently horsed, and the king shown signs of reducing his personal expenditure —in other words, had the trumpets metaphorically been blown less blatantly—other European powers would probably have looked up to England with less respect.

Full well Charles must have known this, for in his way he was thoroughly versed in the art of what is sometimes called "international finessing." His Government knew it better still, with the result that the Government "played up to the king" on the lines adopted by the king in playing up to the Government—both knew that extravagance and display formed the note of the age, and both struck the note firmly with a foot on the loud pedal.

And thus in the reign of the Merry Monarch did the practice that we now sometimes speak of as "bluffing" develop into a sort of art and come to be cultivated carefully.

In the autumn of the seventeenth century Newmarket must truly have been one of the gayest places in England, at anyrate when race meetings were being held there, for it was not unusual for the entire court and cabinet to travel down from London on such occasions, when "jewellers and milliners, players and fiddlers, venal wits and venal beauties would follow in crowds."

Upon such occasions the streets, we are told, were made impassable by coaches and six. "In the places of public resort peers flirted with maids of honour, while officers of the Life Guards, all plumes and gold lace, jostled professors in teachers' caps and black gowns, for from the neighbouring University of Cambridge there always came high functionaries with loyal addresses, and the University would select her ablest theologians to preach before the sovereign and his splendid retinue."

Whether those able theologians were valued at their true worth may be gathered from a further description in which we learn that during the wildest days of the Restoration "the most learned and eloquent divine might fail to draw a fashionable audience, particularly if Buckingham had announced his intention of holding forth, for sometimes his

Grace would enliven the dullness of the Sunday morning by addressing to the bevy of fine gentlemen and fine ladies a ribald exhortation which he called a sermon."

The court of King William, however, proved more decent, and then the Academic dignitaries were treated with marked respect. "Thus with lords and ladies from St James's and Soho, and with doctors from Trinity College and King's College, were mingled the provincial aristocracy, fox-hunting squires and their rosy-cheeked daughters, who had come in queer-looking family coaches drawn by cart horses from the remotest parishes of three or four counties to see their Sovereign.

"The Heath was fringed by a wild, gipsy-like camp of vast extent. For the hope of being able to feed on the leavings of many sumptuous tables, and to pick up some of the guineas and crowns which the spendthrifts of London were throwing about, attracted thousands of peasants from a circle of many miles."

CHAPTER IV

THOUGH James II. strove to emulate to some extent the example set by his lighthearted predecessor on England's throne, he failed almost from the outset to achieve popularity in any marked degree. More partial to hunting than to racing, during his brief reign he nevertheless gave his support to the Turf and strove to encourage the breeding of blood stock. His interest in the chase, however, evaporated almost completely as he became more and more engrossed in the affairs of state.

Whether or no James II. was a finished horseman does not appear, but it may be there is a hidden significance in the statement to be found in several histories that he was "the only crowned head known to have had a surgeon to attend him in the hunting field."

Nor is there evidence of his having ever attended a race meeting after his accession, with the exception of an important meeting held at Winchester in 1685.

The stakes run for at about this time were of small value. Fifty sovereigns were deemed to be a prize well worth winning, while a purse of 100 guineas attracted many

243

spectators and large fields and gave rise to "heated and excited speculation as to the probable results of the contest."

At some of the small meetings valuable horses would be entered to run for a paltry stake of thirty sovereigns, or even for five and twenty, and it was quite common for insignificant races of this kind to be "decided by vile persons."

The weights carried in races run during the latter half of the seventeenth century were out of all proportion. Thus we read of horses carrying ten, twelve and thirteen stone in the final heats of short flat races—in those days almost all races were run in heats. James II. does not appear to have owned any exceptionally famous horses, nor does the horse come prominently to the front during his brief reign of four years.

———————————

Two events of national importance took place in 1689: William and Mary ascended the throne of England, and the famous Byerley Turk, from which so many of our thoroughbred horses are descended, was brought over by his owner, Captain Byerley, who later was to serve in King William's army and fight for him in the battle of the Boyne.

Some say that Captain Byerley had the Turk with him during that battle, but probably this was not so.

From the standpoint from which we are passing the history of this country in review, the arrival of the Byerley Turk was an event of almost as great importance as William and Mary's accession, for as the popularity of the Turf was still increasing year by year the importation of so valuable a stallion as the Byerley Turk in a sense served as a landmark.

And certainly this horse proved to be one of the greatest

of all the sires that were brought over in the seventeenth century. The king, a good judge of a horse, was much attracted by "Byerley's Treasure," as some soon came to call it, and it is known that the king himself owned at this time some of the finest thoroughbreds, probably, that had ever been foaled. That he ran horses of his own at Newmarket is beyond dispute, and the general impression amongst historical writers appears to be that he ran horses also at several other meetings.

It was while attending a race meeting at Newmarket that the king commanded the unjust Act to be put into force which rendered it penal for a Roman Catholic to own a horse worth more than five pounds. Trustworthy historians tell us that most likely the king would not have acted so, but for the influence brought to bear upon him by his queen, who apparently was anxious to vent her spite upon at least one high-born Catholic by whom she had been affronted.

The ultra-bigoted among the king's subjects rejoiced openly at the enforcement of the statute, but, whatever reason there may have been for so severe a measure, the storm of indignation aroused throughout the country caused the king considerable uneasiness.

As a natural result of the enforcement of the Act many Catholics presently substituted teams of oxen, and with these clumsy animals they would drive many miles to attend their church services on Sundays.

How rapidly the Turf must have continued to acquire popularity during this reign is proved by the fact that ten years after the king and queen had ascended the throne—namely, in 1699—more race meetings were held throughout the country than in any previous year in England's history. In this year, too, the King's Master of the Stud, Robert

Marshall, brought over from Arabia fourteen valuable stallions at a cost of some £1100, and these were sent direct to Newmarket, where the king was staying at the time.

That the reports of the evil that is said necessarily to follow in the train of racing were in William's reign greatly exaggerated, as they are to-day, may be gathered from a description of the manners of the age to be found in the diary and state letters of Henry Hyde, Earl of Clarendon.

Hyde, who died at Cornbury, in Oxfordshire, in 1709, at the ripe age of seventy-one, tells us that towards the close of the seventeenth century "a man of the first quality made it his constant practice to go to church," and that he could spend the day in society with his family and friends "without shaking his arm at the gaming-table, associating with jockeys at Newmarket, or murdering time by a constant round of giddy dissipation, if not criminal indulgence."

Other writers make statements practically to the same effect, so it is safe to infer that the foregoing description forms a true account of the style of living in the age when the Turf reached probably its zenith. There are, however, historians who would have us believe that at no period did horse racing flourish in this country without bringing with it, as though by natural process, dissipation, debauchery and general degeneration.

Indeed, as one writer exclaims in an access of unchecked emotion, "from the period when the noble animal became debased and prostituted in this country from the purposes for which he was intended by his Maker—the purposes of war and agriculture—he has gradually sunk, and those who have helped to debase him have at great length followed his example." Out of consideration for this writer's feelings—for it is to be hoped that by now he has recognised the error of his judgment—I refrain from mentioning his name.

William met his death through a riding accident. Mounted upon his favourite "pleasure horse," described as "a steed of mean stature, named Sorrel, which had a blind eye," the king, so it is said, for some reason lost his temper and struck his mount a violent blow upon the head with a heavy riding-stick.

Instantly the animal bounded forward, and William, thrown suddenly off his balance, was unhorsed and fell heavily on his side.

Personally I think the story more likely to be true is that Sorrel stumbled over a molehill, and, in trying to recover himself, fell on to his side. The king, thrown violently, received an internal injury from which he never recovered. Other stories of what took place have also been handed down to us.

No less liberal a supporter of the Turf than William of Orange was Queen Anne, his successor. A modern tautological historian quaintly tells us that "Good Queen Anne had many horses, and they were numerous and costly," a phrase reminiscent of the newspaper reporter's description of a bride's wedding gifts.

That Anne should have loved horses and been an enthusiastic "turfite" is not to be wondered at when we bear in mind the sort of atmosphere in which she had been reared.

The Duke of Cumberland's breeding establishment at Cumberland Lodge in Windsor Great Park—where later on Eclipse and the almost equally famous Herod were to be foaled—probably was the best known in England.

According to Mr Theodore Andrea Cook, our modern authority upon the thoroughbred, its origin, and all that has to do with it, the finest breed of horse ever produced was the result of the cross between the pure Arab and the animal that was in England towards the end of the seventeenth century.

The Darley Arabian, foaled about the month of March, 1702, and his line of distinguished successors, in reality started the long and baffling process which eventually ended in the production of the beautifully shaped animal we see in the modern thoroughbred.

Probably less than fifteen hands, the Darley Arabian was a dark bay descended from the race the most esteemed among the Arabs. Captain Upton maintains that it was of the Ras-el-Fadawi breed, but the mass of the evidence obtainable points rather to its having been a pure Managni.

Certainly the Darley Arabian is one of the most historically interesting horses that has ever been imported into this country. The property of John Brewster Darley, Esq., of Aldby Park, near York, it was bought at Aleppo by Brewster Darley's brother for comparatively a small sum, and sent to England about the year 1705, where subsequently it became the sire of Flying Childers and consequently the great-great-grandsire of Eclipse—three names that stand out in the history of the horse and his connection with the history of this country perhaps more prominently than any other three it would be possible to mention.

Flying Childers, like his sire, was a bay, and Mr Leonard Childers, of Carr House, near Doncaster, who bred him in 1715, soon afterwards sold him to the Duke of Devonshire.

About fourteen and a half hands, Flying Childers is described as "a close-made horse, short-backed and compact, whose reach lay altogether in his limbs."

Eclipse, as we shall see presently, was the reverse of this, for he had great length of waist and stood over much ground.

According to trustworthy statistics, Flying Childers was the fastest horse that ever ran at Newmarket, while it is stated, on what appears to be good authority, that no faster horse has ever lived.

FLYING CHILDERS, BRED BY MR. LEONARD CHILDERS IN 1715, IS SAID TO HAVE BEEN "THE FASTEST HORSE THAT HAS EVER LIVED"

With only Eastern blood in his veins—his dam, Betty

Leedes, was a descendant of pure Eastern horses that had lived long in England—Flying Childers' career upon the Turf was truly phenomenal. He died in 1741.

———————

Another historic sire of the early part of the eighteenth century was the Godolphin Arabian, called also the Godolphin Barb, foaled in 1724.

His height was about fifteen hands, and his colour a dark brown.

We are told that he was sent to Louis XIV. by the Emperor of Morocco, but it is known that when he died he belonged to the Earl of Godolphin.

Whether the pedigrees of all modern thoroughbreds can or cannot be traced back to the Byerley Turk, to the Darley Arabian, or to the Godolphin Arabian, is still a source of argument, and opinions upon the point probably are about equally divided.

A romantic story attaches to the Godolphin Barb—to the last he was pronounced by Lord Godolphin to be an Arabian—inasmuch as he was at one period of his life driven in a water cart in the streets of Paris. He died in 1753, and his remains lie under the stable gateway at Gog Magog, near Cambridge.

———————

After the race meeting known as Royal Ascot had been inaugurated by Queen Anne, in 1712, the tone of the Turf in England greatly improved. The rules of racing were revised, and more attention was paid to their enforcement. Also steps were taken to prevent "undesirable and roguish persons" from "indulging in their wicked and thievish habits"—in short, a serious attempt was made to purify the Turf, as the process is termed now.

To what extent this alleged purification proved effectual we are not told, but a number of persons who probably were considered "undesirable and roguish," were, about the year 1718, ordered to "abstain from attending the meetings," a command that most likely was the equivalent for being warned off the Turf, and apparently is the first actual allusion to warning off the Turf that is to be found mentioned in history. It has even been maintained that the inauguration of the Jockey Club, believed to have taken place in 1750, was prompted by an urgent necessity for a body of responsible Turf administrators with power "to order thievish persons to keep away."

I believe it is not generally known, except among persons versed in Turf history, that prior to the inauguration of the Derby and the Oaks it was quite exceptional for three-year-old horses to be raced at all. Before that time the three-year-old was looked upon more or less in the same way that to-day we look upon the yearling.

Indeed early in the eighteenth century but few horses were run when very young. In William and Mary's reign some of the most important races were won by six-year-olds, and we find allusion to a six-year-old plate that must have been run for at about this time. Nearly all the long races were still run in heats, and some of the horses entered were nine, ten, twelve and even more.

—————

The practice of cropping manes and docking tails was

expressly condemned by Queen Anne, also by one of the Georges, probably George III. Berenger, in his "History and Art of Horsemanship," published in 1771, observes that "the cruelty and absurdity of our notions and customs in 'cropping,' as it is called, the ears of our horses, 'docking' and 'nicking' their tails, is such that we every day fly in the face of reason, nature and humanity.

"Nor is the existing race of men in this island alone to be charged with this folly, almost unbecoming the ignorance and cruelty of savages, but their forefathers several centuries ago were charged and reprehended by a public canon for this absurd and barbarous practice.

"However, we need but look into the streets and roads to be convinced that their descendants have not degenerated from them, although his present Majesty in his wisdom and humanity has endeavoured to reclaim them by issuing an order that the horses which serve in his troops shall remain as nature designed them."

Only a few years after the publication of the "History and Art of Horsemanship" a determined attempt was made to suppress, once and for all time, the practices referred to. For a while public interest was greatly stirred, and it seemed as though the practices would at last be put an end to by direct legislation, but eventually undue influence was brought to bear, and nothing was done.

Indeed, as most of us must have noticed, the practice of docking the tails of nearly all horses except race horses is so prevalent at the present time that in many instances the tails are cut to within a few inches of the root, while some of our ultra "fashionable" horse dealers go so far as to pluck out most of the hairs left on the stump.

In the west of England the latter trick is indulged in more

often than in the northern counties or the midlands.

———————————

Of all the famous sires whose names stand out as household words in the annals of the horse in history, but few bear comparison with the world-renowned Eclipse.

MR. O'KELLY'S ECLIPSE, THE MOST FAMOUS THOROUGHBRED
STALLION EVER FOALED 1764
After the painting by G. Stubbs

Bred, as already mentioned, by the Duke of Cumberland, he took his name from the coincidence that the great eclipse of 1764 was in progress at the very hour of his birth.

There does not seem to have been anything particularly striking about the foal's appearance, and certainly none imagined for a moment that he would be likely to grow into one of the most famous horses, if not the most famous horse, the Turf has ever known.

Until the age of five, Eclipse was not run in public, but from the time he won his first race, in May 1769, until his last appearance upon the Turf, in October 1770, he was never beaten, or near being beaten. The long list of his triumphs need not be given here, but Mr Theodore Cook reminds us in his exhaustive work upon this horse that it was Dennis O'Kelly's son of Eclipse that won the second Derby, and that out of 127 races, including the first, Eclipse's descendants had down to the year 1906 furnished no fewer than eighty-two winners.

Eclipse himself was sold as a yearling for less than 100 guineas. Of his direct descendants, a yearling filly was bought not very long ago for 10,000 guineas; a race horse in training has fetched £39,375 at public auction; two sires have each produced stock that has won over half-a-million sterling; and other horses tracing back to him in the direct male line have won the "Triple Crown" nine times out of ten and hold the record for the pace at which the Two-Thousand, the Derby and the Leger have been run.

Upon one point all trustworthy authorities on thoroughbreds and their performances, also the principal historians of the Turf, and in addition the leading "turfites" of our own period, are in agreement, and that is that since the time of Flying Childers the Turf, the world over, has not known a horse faster than Eclipse was.

This in itself is exceptional praise, but Eclipse was to add materially to his extraordinary reputation, for while at stud he became the sire of 335 winners who between the year 1774 and the year 1796 won close upon £160,000 in stakes alone, exclusive of cups and plates, and in addition his owner is known to have stated openly that he was paid for the horse's services as a stallion upwards of £25,000.

Referring again to the later descendants of Eclipse, we find that in the year 1894 they won between them over £421,400 in stakes, the number of winners being 827, and the total number of races won, 1469. Indeed there probably is not any other horse in the world, nor ever has been, that has been the prime cause of so much money changing hands.

Perhaps what most attracted attention to Eclipse in his racing days was the apparent ease with which he won. His stride is said to have been phenomenal. Did he, during the whole of his career upon the Turf, ever fully extend himself? The question has many times been discussed by experts, and the consensus of opinion seems to point to the conclusion that he never did.

For even after making his greatest efforts he did not seem to be distressed. The race-loving public seemed almost to worship him at about the period he reached his zenith, and in the end it was to all intents impossible to back him.

The interest the king was known to take in Eclipse was very great, yet probably George III. was at heart less interested in the sport of racing than any of his predecessors had been.

Thackeray insinuates this in his immortal satire of "The Four Georges," and with truth it may be said that of all the great horses that have figured prominently either directly or indirectly in the history of this country, Flying Childers and Eclipse take precedence.

Much that has been written on the subject of Queen Anne's alleged fondness for horses would seem to be based on doubtful knowledge. The more discriminating among our historians appear to think that too much importance has been attached to many of the statements.

There are, I believe, letters extant from Queen Anne in which she talks at length upon the subject of the horses that belonged to her, but certain documents of the same sort are attributed to her which she probably did not write.

The King of Denmark, upon one occasion made her a present of twelve mares carefully chosen by himself, but for the rest the majority of the stories told of Queen Anne should be accepted with reservation.

Indeed from the middle of the eighteenth to the middle of the nineteenth century the horse again figured largely in romance, a fact that may in a measure account for the stories that have been put about of Queen Anne and her horses.

Smollett is but one of the writers whose works are prolific of narratives of the kind, and some of these stories from being repeated so frequently came at last to be believed by a mass of the people.

Thus the tales of Sir Launcelot Graves' adventures, and of the acts that were attributed to Sir Launcelot's grotesque "mettlesome sorrel," Bronzomarte, were believed by some actually to be true.

In point of fact this Sir Launcelot must have been a sort of Don Quixote who in the reign of George II. deemed it his mission to roam about England "redressing wrongs, discouraging moral evils not recognisable by law, degrading immodesty, punishing ingratitude and reforming society generally."

Fables were related too of Robert Burns' mare, Jenny Geddes, while the poets also took possession of the palfrey which belonged to Madame Chatelet of Circy—the lady with whom Voltaire lived for ten or more years—and wove around it, also round its mistress, many romantic but wholly fictitious narratives.

Its name was Rossignol, and, according to one poet at least, Madame Chatelet fed the creature "on newly picked apricots, gave it milk to drink, and rode with a silken rein." Rossignol is mentioned also in the history of Voltaire's life.

The story of Dr Dove's steed that was called Nobbs has the seal of Southey upon it, which may account for the animal's having been dragged into so many romances. At best, however, it was a foolish beast. Dr Dove, it may be unnecessary to remind the reader, is the hero of Southey's "Doctor." The extent to which some of the famous stories of romance came in course of time to be woven into other stories is rather remarkable.

Thus we find Dr Dove described in three different stories as three distinct and different individuals not one of whom is recognisable as the same person and the original, while the horse, Nobbs, is spoken of in one story as a bay, in another as a brown, in a third as a black.

Is it possible that the authors of those stories can have read the original Southey? And if history of such small importance, comparatively, is thus corrupted, can one place implicit belief in many of the serious historical narratives? Rather one is tempted to believe the assertion of Pitt, "the boy Prime Minister," when he declared in all seriousness that "nothing is so uncertain as positive truth."

Most historians make mention of the charger that carried Wellington so well at Waterloo; yet the only statement with the impress of truth in this connection is that the horse died in 1835, aged twenty-seven. It was Wellington's favourite steed, and its name was Copenhagen. Of his other horses we read but little.

Marengo, Napoleon's favourite mount, was, according to one historian, a pure white stallion; according to another a cream-coloured gelding. In Vernet's famous picture of Napoleon crossing the Alps we are shown a snow-white horse, and Meissonnier shows us a snow-white horse too, so most likely this animal actually was quite white. The resting-place of Marengo's remains is the Museum of the United Services, in London.

NAPOLEON AT WAGRAM
From the famous painting by Vernet at Versailles

In an age when attempts are made to overthrow almost every established historical record, and when we are even informed quite gravely that Joan of Arc was not burnt at the stake at all, but that the victim was some other woman —a lady of rank, who out of compassion for the poor Pucelle was at the last moment prompted to sacrifice herself in her place!—it is not surprising that sceptics should exist who would have us believe that Napoleon's horse was not called Marengo.

What is it, precisely, that prompts this section of modern searchers after "positive truth" to cast doubts upon so many of the minor historical incidents? For, as a reviewer recently observed, it is hardly worth the while of any serious historian to waste time in refuting such misstatements.

Sir Charles Napier owned a mare that he prized greatly. Its name was Molly, but it does not appear to have performed any exceptional feats of prowess. Apparently the only point about it upon which our historians lay stress is that the animal lived to the age of five and thirty. As for Lord Nelson's connection with horses, so far as I have been able to ascertain it was limited to his superstitious belief that the possession of a horseshoe must bring him luck. At any rate he always kept at least one horseshoe nailed to the mast of his ship, the *Victory*.

The story of Siegfried's horse, Grane, is of course well known. In William Combe's quaint tale of the simple-minded, henpecked clergyman, Dr Syntax, we have a horse named Grizzle that was "all skin and bone." Written in eight-syllable verse, the narrative explains in rather an amusing way how the eccentric old scholar left home in search of the picturesque, and Grizzle figures largely in it from beginning to end, in much the same way that the ill-starred pony, Fiddleback, figures in Goldsmith's narrative.

WELLINGTON'S FAMOUS HORSE, COPENHAGEN

CHAPTER V

WITH the early years of our reigning sovereign's period the long story of the horse's progress through history may be deemed to have come practically to an end.

We have seen how the very early races of Asia, of Africa, and of Europe were enabled to spread their power, and were assisted in protecting themselves against the onslaughts of their numerous enemies, by possessing many horses upon which they could depend implicitly in the hour of strife.

The Egyptians, Medes, Persians, Syrians, Scythians, Libyans, Carthaginians, Macedonians, Numidians—all owed their series of successes in a great measure to the fact that they owned horses when their antagonists either had none at all, or else only a few, and those of an indifferent stamp.

Thus through the whole course of history the influence of the horse can be traced.

Rome, until after the conquest of Gaul, was deemed a weak nation in some respects, and when we study the history of Rome at about that period we find the weakness to have been in a measure attributable to Rome's shortage of horses during the greater part of that long spell.

Coming to what has been termed the Arabian period, history proves beyond all doubt that the spread of Islam was due partly to the Arabians having at about that time become possessors of many horses.

Indeed had the Franks not owned a great number of exceptionally fine horses by about the beginning of the sixth century A.D., who can say that the Saracens would not, after the year 732 A.D., have vanquished the larger portion of Western Europe?

Again, what chance of victory would the Normans have had at Hastings had Harold's forces been mounted on horseback? For when we remember the valiant way that Harold and his men fought it is easy to believe that the Normans would have been completely routed had they too been fighting on foot and not on horseback, in which case the entire history of this country would very likely have been different.

━━━━━━━━

In the Middle Ages we find the horse playing if possible a more important part in the making of history than it had done in the previous centuries, for what would have become of England's power, and her prestige, had she been deprived of those great war horses and the almost invulnerable men-at-arms who bestrode them?

England's might spread steadily while the strength and size of her horses went on increasing, and while the weight of the armour worn by horses and men grew gradually heavier and heavier.

The limit in weight of armour would appear to have been reached when a horse became compelled to carry a man and armour that weighed together between thirty and three and thirty stone.

It was soon after this limit had been arrived at that the era of the new and armourless cavalry-man mounted on a light and active horse set in unexpectedly.

Coming to more recent years, what would Marlborough or any other of the great and successful military leaders have done had they been deprived of even a portion of their cavalry?

With the outbreak of the Boer War the wise-acres shook their heads, declaring that in such a country as South Africa the mounted soldier must prove useless; that the "punitive expedition," as the campaign was termed when first war was declared, would be conducted almost solely by infantry; while reasons innumerable were advanced to prove the "accuracy" of such wild forecasts.

And now when we look back upon it all we see that the war would most likely still be dragging its way along had only infantry been employed.

———————

To-day it seems likely, indeed almost certain, that the horse's influence upon the world's progress—influence that we have traced back into the dim ages—has actually come to a close.

Evidence that this is so is observable on every side. The discovery of the strength of steam left the horse still in power, so to speak, for the locomotive engine drove only coach horses out of existence.

The utility of the electrically driven motor, and of the motor driven by petrol power, has been proved to be almost ubiquitous, and the rapidity with which the motor has already ousted horses in almost every direction is little short of phenomenal.

For the ultra-conservative little body of the community to maintain that this is not so because it hates to speak or think of automobiles comes near to being grotesque. We are confronted by hard facts that cannot be avoided, and whether we like them or not they nevertheless must force us to realise what is happening.

FLYING DUTCHMAN. FOALED 1846
From a life-size painting by Herring

Shall I be charged with indulging a flight of imagination if I venture to declare that, before three decades more have passed, the horse will have become so completely dethroned that it will be with us only for racing purposes and to assist us in the artificial chase?

If about the year 2030 some student of past history shall come upon these lines I trust that he will quote them with appropriate comment.

Horses famous in history other than that of the Turf occur but rarely in the records of the last century or so. Lord Cardigan had a chestnut thoroughbred that carried him unscathed through the memorable Balaclava Charge, but there does not appear to be any story of interest attaching to the animal—it had two white stockings and its name was Ronald.

I have tried to trace the origin of the superstitious belief that the possession of a horseshoe must bring luck, but without any very satisfactory result. The superstition reached its height apparently towards the middle of the eighteenth century, or a little later, and by the middle of the nineteenth it was steadily dying out.

A horseshoe nailed to a house door was in the first instance supposed to keep away witches, a belief which gradually developed into the supposition that the possession of the shoe would in some way bring good fortune to the owner. According to several writers, most of the houses in the west end of London at one time had a horseshoe on the threshold, and it is said that in the year 1813 no less than seventeen shoes nailed to doors were to be seen in Monmouth Street alone.

Also it is asserted that as late as the year 1855 seven horseshoes remained nailed to different doors in that street alone.

———————————

In his interesting book, "Bedouin Tribes of the Euphrates," Mr Blunt has something to say upon the subject of the treatment of horses by the Bedouins.

The Bedouin, it seems, as a rule does not use either bit or bridle, but controls his horse by means of a halter to which a thin chain is attached that passes round the nose.

Apparently stirrups are unknown to the Bedouin, while in place of a saddle he uses a stout pad made of cotton which he binds on to the horse's back with the help of a surcingle.

Among the many interesting statements in this book is one to the effect that the Bedouin cannot ascertain a horse's age by examining the teeth, and that he has no knowledge of the trick so often resorted to by unprincipled European horse dealers of making false marks on teeth.

Many Chinamen, on the other hand, claim to be able to tell a horse's age from its teeth up to the age of thirty-two.

A point omitted by Mr Blunt is that the Bedouin being, so to speak, born a horseman, is unable to understand how any race of men can exist that cannot ride. Were we to be told that a race of men exist who have never learnt to walk we should be about as much surprised as the Bedouin is.

Our leading authorities upon the history of the thoroughbred are unanimous in asserting that until about a century and a half ago the thoroughbred was unknown in America.

Yet among the famous descendants of the first thoroughbreds imported into the United States we find horses of world-wide renown, such animals, for instance, as Iroquois and Foxhall. These two horses are especially worthy of mention, inasmuch as they achieved success that came near to being phenomenal.

How remarkable the development of the thoroughbred has been in our own country may be gathered from our knowledge that whereas the fee charge for the services of Herod at stud was but ten guineas, and for Touchstone only sixty guineas, to-day the fee for the use of a "fashionable" stallion is frequently from 500 to 600 guineas.

The Committee of the House of Lords that met in the year 1873 to discuss the question of horse breeding did much to encourage the rearing of the very best stock obtainable. The famous race horse, Common, by Isonomy out of Thistle, bred in 1888, made his first appearance as a three-year-old and won for Lord Arlington and Sir Frederick Johnson — his joint owners—the Two Thousand, the Derby and the Leger, a performance that at once places him in one of the most important niches of fame in the latter part of the last century.

Another of the "immortals" who won the three great races is Gladiateur, a name that recalls to mind a host of thoroughbreds whose fame will be handed down to posterity—Blue Gown, Blair Athol, Harkaway, Ormonde, St Gatien, Robert the Devil, Hermit, Persimmon, Flying Fox, Donovan—the names come tumbling into one's thoughts pell mell; but as the triumphs of these and many other giants of the turf of comparatively modern times have been described in detail again and again in the many volumes devoted to the thoroughbred and his history, they need not be repeated here.

Yet it is worthy of mention that though some few years ago the famous thoroughbred sires in this country included 260 direct descendants of Eclipse, and sixty direct descendants of the Byerley Turk, they included only thirty-six direct descendants of the greatly glorified Godolphin Arabian.

I believe I am right in saying that the cream-white horses

which, until comparatively a recent date, were used by the king on state occasions, are directly descended from the celebrated white horses formerly in the royal stables at Hanover.

Allusion to these animals recalls to mind a method of controlling horses that is said to be in vogue still in parts of Austria, where it is spoken of as "the Balassiren" of horses, and that in reality is a method of mesmerising horses before shoeing them.

According to Obersteimer, whose words are quoted in Hudson's "Psychic Phenomena," the process takes its name from a cavalry officer named Balassa, who was the first to introduce or to attempt it.

Under the circumstances it is interesting to read that among the early Egyptians there were men who could, or who professed to be able to, obtain complete control over horses and other animals by the exercise solely of will power, and that such men were sometimes called in upon occasions when a horse had to be bound.

It therefore seems possible that some at least of the horses sacrificed in the ages before Christ may first have been dazed, if not rendered unconscious, with the aid of some such agency as hypnotism.

Though the Derby and the Oaks were not inaugurated until the last quarter of the eighteenth century—when, as Lord Rosebery tells us, "a roystering party at a country house founded two races and named them gratefully after their host and his house"—horse racing has now for many years been popular in nearly every civilised country, while in some of the uncivilised countries it has long been

269

included among the favourite pastimes of the people.

Thus Mr C. W. Campbell, H. M. Consul at Wuchow before 1904, mentions in the report of a journey that he made through Mongolia that the Mongols are extremely fond of racing. He adds, however, that the practice of betting upon horse races was almost unknown there at the time he wrote, and goes on to say that in the Chahar country an ounce or two of silver—worth at most from two shillings to half-a-crown—was in some instances the only prize offered, though plenty of the races were run over a ten-mile course!

According to Mr Campbell, the Derby of Mongolia is held near Urga, under the direct patronage of the Bogdo. The course is thirty miles in length, and much of it rough steppe, and "the winners are presented to the Bogdo, who maintains them for the rest of their lives in honourable idleness."

The jockeys are the smallest boys able to ride the distance. "A saddle or seat aid in any form is not allowed. The jockeys simply roll up their loose cotton trousers as high as they can, clutch the pony's ribs with their bare legs, and all carry long whips. The bridles—single snaffles with rawhide reins —have each a round disc of burnished silver attached to the headband."

What will happen in the future when the horse shall have become practically extinct in the civilised countries? The question is exercising the minds of many as these lines are being written. There are some who cling still to the belief that the horse's day is not over, indeed that it never will be over, but unfortunately they are visionaries able to believe that which they so ardently wish.

For as Mr W. Phillpotts Williams, the energetic founder of the Brood Mare Society, pointed out in June last (1908), the idea suggested recently of giving to farmers in this country a bonus for the possession of young horses suitable for artillery mounts would never have the effect of keeping horses in this country. All it would do, as he says, would be to collect the horses at the English tax-payers' expense for the foreigner to buy. The horses would be kept by the English farmer through the risky years of youth, only to be bought, when matured and fit, by the buyers for the foreign armies.

Give a farmer £5 a year. The foreigner has only to add £5 to the horse's value, and away it will go. What is needed, as Mr Williams truly remarks—and none knows better the existing condition of affairs in this respect at the present time—is drastic action at the ports for horses bred under such a grant, while in any and every scheme that may be tried all the government-bred stock ought to be ear-marked and kept strictly in the country.

One of the Belgian officers who visited England officially some months ago incidentally mentioned that the Belgian government has dealers in Ireland who are commissioned to send over to the Belgian army a large supply of horses annually. "Practically all our army horses are Irish," he said. From this statement we may well assume that it would be possible to breed at a profit, in Ireland, a very large number of horses annually. Probably no country in the world is better suited than Ireland for horse breeding. Yet the shrinkage in the reserve of horses in Great Britain continues practically unchecked, and, according to statistics, a month or two ago one of the largest of the omnibus companies in London was selling off its horses at the rate of a hundred or so a a week!

As a natural result of all this, the demand for oats has recently fallen by more than twenty per cent. The Board of Agriculture believes that the retention of colts is all that matters, while the Royal Commission, to judge from their annual report, apparently labour under the mistaken impression that the supply of thoroughbred sires must solve the difficulty of keeping up the supply of horses.

Without in the least wishing to be pessimistic, therefore, one must look facts in the face, and, looking them in the face, one cannot do otherwise than admit regretfully enough that the long and glorious career of the horse in its direct and indirect bearing upon the development of the world and the progress of civilisation has at last come somewhat abruptly to a close.

INDEX

in Middle Ages, 114;
in the sixteenth century, 141;
the seventeenth century, 257;
Cardinal Wolsey's interest in, 143

Bridles, 51, 64, 135, 237, 286, 291

Bronze Age, the, 4, 6, 16, 17

Bronze of Alexander, 61

Bronze horse in British Museum, 64

Brood Mare Society, 292

Bucephalus, 54, 61

"Byerley Turk," the, 215, 263, 289

CALIGULA'S horse—a priest, 79

Carey's ride, Sir Robert, 197, 198

"Carmen," 135

Cart horses, 207, 236

Cauldrons and tripods, 11

Cavalry, 16, 22, 23, 46, 199, 283, 292;
Assyrian, 9;
British, 67, 68;
Cromwell's, 233, 234;
described by Julius Cæsar, 70, 71;
first use of, 7;
Greek, 9, 22;
Hannibal's, 64, 65, 69;
Henry II.'s, 111;
Iberian, 65;
Persian, 114;
Richard II.'s opinion of, 131;
superseded chariots, 74;

287

Horse thieves, 120

Hunters, 183, 207

Hunting 118, 161, 162, 179, 180, 187, 192, 218, 241, 253, 261

Huntingdon, race at, 220

Hyde Park Meeting, 224

"Hyksos, The," 2

Hypanis, the (River Bug), 21

Hyperenor, 12

Hypnotism of horses, 289-290

Iceni, the, 75, 117

Ill-treatment of horses, 100, 105, 129, 271, 272

India, 36

Influence of the horse on history, 96, 97, 103, 104, 183, 281-284

Ireland, 17, 18, 74, 75, 115, 116, 252

Iron Age, the, 15, 17, 19, 22

"Iron Horseman, An," 227

"Isokelismos," 30

James I., at Lincoln, 219;
    encouraged gambling, 210;
    improvement of horses under, 203;
    liked tall horses, 215;
    love of racing, 202, 209, 210;
    made Newmarket "a royal village," 205;
    present of horses from Naples, 207;
    Royal studs of, 207;

Gradasso's, 94;
Henry VIII.'s, 165;
Mahomet's, 88;
Mary Queen of Scots', 189;
of the ancients, 97;
Richard II.'s, 128;
Roderick's, 93;
William the Conqueror's, 108;
Xenophon's, 38, 48

Wheels of chariots, 20

White animals sacred, 33, 36

White hoof, a, 214

White horse, the, 21, 31, 32;
    banner of, 69, 91, 92;
    beloved of the gods, 33, 122;
    criminal act to wound a, 123;
    divination by sacred, 79;
    Joan of Arc's, 137, 138;
    Mahomet's Alborak, 89;
    Napoleon's, 279;
    not liked for work, 67;
    of Chinghas Khan, 121-123;
    of the Scandinavians, 95;
    of Selene, 98, 99;
    sacrificed, 33, 36, 50, 78, 123;
    superstitions about, 123;
    stud of Richard III., 139;
    "White Surrey" of Richard III., 139;
    "White Turk," of Cromwell, 279

William the Conqueror, 97, 103, 108-110, 114

William III., Acts against Roman Catholics possessing
  horses, 264;
    for development of horses, 153;
    court of, 259;
    interest in horses, 263-266;
    statue in Dublin, 236, 237

William Stephanides, 110

Winchester Meeting, the, 262

Windsor Great Park, 267

Windsor, stud at, 125

THE RIVERSIDE PRESS LIMITED, EDINBURGH.